FIRST
TO
FLY

Also by Charles Bracelen Flood

Love Is a Bridge

A Distant Drum

Tell Me, Stranger

Monmouth

More Lives Than One

The War of the Innocents

Trouble at the Top

*Rise, and Fight Again: Perilous Times Along
the Road to Independence*

Lee: The Last Years

Hitler: The Path to Power

Der Kaufmann von Canossa

*Grant and Sherman: The Friendship That
Won the Civil War*

1864: Lincoln at the Gates of History

*Grant's Final Victory: Ulysses S. Grant's
Heroic Last Year*

FIRST
TO
FLY

The Story of the Lafayette Escadrille,
the American Heroes
Who Flew for France in World War I

CHARLES BRACELEN FLOOD

Atlantic Monthly Press
New York

Published simultaneously in Canada
Printed in the United States of America

FIRST EDITION

ISBN 978-0-8021-2365-7
eISBN 978-0-8021-9138-0

Atlantic Monthly Press
an imprint of Grove Atlantic
154 West 14th Street
New York, NY 10011

Distributed by Publishers Group West

groveatlantic.com

15 16 17 18   10 9 8 7 6 5 4 3 2 1

Oh! I have slipped the surly bonds of Earth,
And danced the skies on laughter-silvered wings;
Sunward I've climbed and joined the tumbling mirth
Of sun-split clouds—and done a hundred things
You have not dreamed of—wheeled and soared and swung
High in the sunlit silence.
Hov'ring there
I've chased the shouting wind along and flung
My eager craft through footless halls of air . . .

Up, up the long, delirious burning blue
I've topped the wind-swept heights with easy grace
Where never lark, or even eagle flew—
And, while with silent, lifting mind I've trod
The high untrespassed sanctity of space,
Put out my hand and touched the face of God.

—*High Flight* by pilot John Gillespie Magee Jr.,
killed at age nineteen

"We Americans who had enjoyed the hospitality of France, and had learned to love the country and the people, simply had to fight. Our consciences demanded it."

—An American volunteer pilot, about his
determination to fight for France

Dramatis Personae

JULES JAMES "JIMMY" BACH, aerodynamics expert from New Orleans who became one of the first Americans to join the French Foreign Legion

CLYDE BALSLEY, American fighter pilot from Texas

OSWALD BOELCKE, Baron Manfred von Richthofen's mentor and tutor

ARISTIDE BRIAND, prime minister of France

EUGENE BULLARD, first black fighter pilot

VICTOR CHAPMAN, beloved fighter pilot from New York

"CHER AMI," heroic messenger pigeon that saved the remnants of the "Lost Battalion"

ELLIOT COWDIN, polo player from Long Island who lobbied the French government for the creation of an American squadron

YVONNE DACREE, young Frenchwoman and Bert Hall's love interest

EDMOND GENET, youngest Escadrille pilot; deserter from the United States Navy; brave, gifted, and in effect an American spy within the French Air Service

HERMANN GOERING, German ace, future number two Nazi and reichsmarschall in command of the Luftwaffe in World War Two

DR. EDMUND GROS, originally from San Francisco, prominent expatriate who helped raise funds to create the Lafayette Escadrille

JAMES NORMAN HALL, future author of *Mutiny on the Bounty*

WESTON "BERT" HALL, the Escadrille's controversial man of mystery

MATA HARI, Dutch exotic dancer and German spy; executed by the French

MYRON T. HERRICK, American ambassador to France

RAOUL LUFBERY, Escadrille's leading ace

KENNETH MARR, gifted pilot and adventurer from California

CHARLES NUNGESSER, most colorful of the great French aces, twice attached to fly with the Escadrille

EDWIN "NED" PARSONS, future ace and author of Escadrille memoirs, from Holyoke, Massachusetts

PAUL PAVELKA, adventurer and repeated volunteer who fought around the world

GENERAL JOHN J. PERSHING, commander of the American Expeditionary Force

NORMAN PRINCE, rich, bilingual, well-connected young pilot from Massachusetts, instrumental in creating the Escadrille

BARON MANFRED VON RICHTHOFEN, "The Red Baron," commander of the "Flying Circus" and the war's leading ace, with eighty Allied planes shot down

EDDIE RICKENBACKER, leading ace of the United States Army pilots after America came into the war

KIFFIN AND PAUL ROCKWELL, brothers from North Carolina who enlisted in the French Foreign Legion before the Escadrille

BILL THAW, the Escadrille's de facto American leader

GEORGES THENAULT, French commander of the Lafayette Escadrille

ERNST UDET, famous German ace

ALICE WEEKS, rich American who devoted herself to taking care of American military men in Paris, including Escadrille pilots

HAROLD WILLIS, ex-Harvard football player and valuable Escadrille pilot from Boston

WHISKEY AND SODA, Escadrille's lion cub mascots

Chronology

The First World War, Interspersed with Important Lafayette Escadrille–Related Dates

1914

> August 2. Germany invades France.
> August 4. United Kingdom declares war on Germany.
> **August 21. Paul and Kiffin Rockwell from North Carolina join the French Foreign Legion in Paris. Kiffin goes on to be an Escadrille pilot.
> September 5. First Battle of the Marne begins.
> October 19. Battle of Ypres begins.

1915

> February 19. Dardanelles Campaign begins.
> April 22. Second Battle of Ypres begins.
> April 25. The Battle of Gallipoli begins.
> **September 23. Pilot Jimmy Bach flies spy mission, is captured, and becomes the Germans' first American prisoner of war.
> **December 23. Pilots William Thaw, Norman Prince, and Eliot Cowdin arrive in Manhattan for a Christmas leave that proves to be a propaganda victory for the French cause.

1916

February 21. Battle of Verdun begins.

**April 20. First members of the *Escadrille Americaine* (American Squadron) arrive at the airfield at Luxueil-les-Bains. They are commanded by Captain Georges Thenault of the French Army.

**May 18. Kiffin Rockwell becomes first volunteer American pilot to shoot down a German plane.

**May 20. Squadron leaves for Bar-le-Duc, to support the Battle of Verdun.

**June 18. Pilot Clyde Balsley is shot down and critically wounded. He will be in French hospitals for nineteen months.

**June 23. Pilot Victor Chapman is shot down and killed. Thus in one week the Escadrille suffers its first wounding and death.

July 2. Battle of the Somme begins.

**September 23. Kiffin Rockwell is killed in action.

**October 12. Squadron participates in historic Allied bombing raid on the arms factory at Oberndorf, Germany, which was sending ten thousand rifles a day to the Western Front. Some record this as the birth of strategic bombing. Pilot Norman Prince is mortally injured in a landing accident returning from the raid, and dies three days later.

**December 6. Squadron is officially renamed the *Lafayette Escadrille*.

**mid-December. Pilot Weston "Bert" Hall leaves the Escadrille to begin special missions in Romania and Russia.

1917

April 8. United States enters the war.

**April 16. Pilot Edmond Genet is killed in action.

June 26. First U.S. Army troops arrive in France.

July 31. Battle of Passchendaele begins.

**August 18. Pilot Harold Willis is shot down and captured. He will escape from a prison camp and reach Paris at the end of the war.

September 4. First U.S. Army troops are killed in action.

November 7. Bolsheviks seize power in Russia.

**November 11. Pilot Paul Pavelka is killed in freak horseback accident at Salonika.

December 17. New Russian government signs armistice with Germany and its allies.

1918

**February 18. Lafayette Escadrille is officially dissolved. Most of its pilots transfer to the United States Army Air Service.

March 21. Germany begins Spring Offensive.

**April 21. Germany's Manfred von Richthofen, the Red Baron, the war's greatest ace, is shot down and killed.

May 18. First U.S. Army offensive—Battle of Cantigny.

**May 19. Escadrille ace pilot Raoul Lufbery is killed in action.

August 6. American troops begin Battle of Chateau-Thierry and the Aisne-Marne operation.

September 12. U.S. Army begins Meuse-Argonne offensive, including the Battle of St. Mihiel.

November 9. German Kaiser Wilhelm abdicates and flees to Holland.

November 11. First World War ends.

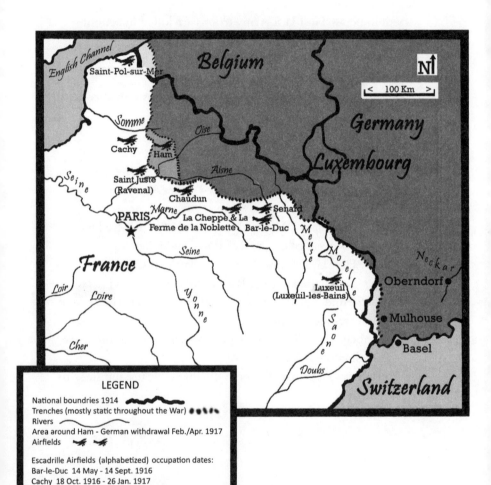

English Channel
Saint-Pol-sur-Mer
Belgium
Germany
Luxembourg

N↑
|< 100 Km >|

Somme
Oise
Cachy
Ham
Aisne
Seine
Saint Juste
(Ravenal)
Chaudun
Marne
Senard
PARIS
La Cheppe & La
Ferme de la Noblette
Bar-le-Duc
Meuse
Moselle
Neckar
France
Seine
Oberndorf
Loir
Loire
Yonne
Luxeuil
(Luxeuil-les-Bains)
Saone
Mulhouse
Cher
Basel
Doubs
Switzerland

LEGEND

National boundries 1914 ～～～
Trenches (mostly static throughout the War) ●●●●●
Rivers
Area around Ham - German withdrawal Feb./Apr. 1917
Airfields ✈ ✈

Escadrille Airfields (alphabetized) occupation dates:
Bar-le-Duc 14 May - 14 Sept. 1916
Cachy 18 Oct. 1916 - 26 Jan. 1917
Chaudun 3 June - 17 July & 20 Sept. - 3 Dec. 1917
Ham 7 April - 3 June 1917
La Cheppe & Ferme de la Noblette 3 Dec. 1918
Luxeuil 20 April - 19 May &14 Sept. - 18 Oct. 1916
Saint Juste (Ravenal) 26 Jan. - 7 April 1917
Saint Pol sur Mer 17 July - 11 August 1917
Senard 11 Aug. - 28 Sept. 1917

Table of Contents

FIRST
TO
FLY

Introduction

Two Deaths Trigger Thirty-seven Million More

On Sunday, June 28, 1914, an inconspicuous nineteen-year-old Serbian terrorist named Gavrilo Princip, shot and killed Archduke Ferdinand of Austria and his wife, Sophie, during their state visit to the Bosnian capital of Sarajevo.

Across the month of July, the assassination embroiled the chancelleries of Europe in an escalating series of misperceptions and miscalculations. Austria-Hungary asked Germany if it would support their desire to punish Serbia for the murders. The Germans promptly said they would, even if Russia backed the Serbians. When Moscow warned against invading Serbia, France was drawn into the rising hostilities by her treaty with Russia. Last came the British, who had a treaty with France. By August, thousands of men were dying on a dozen battlefields.

That militaristic belief had fostered a German expansionist policy that caused other European nations to form defensive alliances that the Germans denounced as "encirclement."The Allied armies, rapidly mobilizing amid the diplomatic turmoil, were those of the British Empire, France, Italy, and Russia.

Germany invaded France on August 2, 1914, and declared war on France a day later.The Germans had already declared war on Russia on August 1, and declared war on Belgium on August 4.The swift German advances brought England and the British Empire, including the forces of Canada and Australia, into the war on August 4. By the end of August, Germany was engaged in an all-out, two-front war, fighting the French, Belgian, and British armies on the Western Front, and a large principally Russian force on the Eastern Front. Both sides believed that they would win the war by Christmas.

The United States remained neutral, and would not become officially involved for close to three years, but scores of American men and women soon made their way into European battle zones. Their motivations combined idealism and a thirst for adventure, and their stories were of courage and newly discovered skills.

Of all the personal experiences that occurred during the enormous four-year struggle that became known as the Great War, the most spectacular involved aerial warfare, with pilots on both sides using new weapons in a new dimension.Their duels in the sky evoked centuries-old images of knights on horseback engaging in tournaments.

At the war's outset, Americans who wished to serve the French cause had to confront the American policy that, as citizens of a neutral nation, it was illegal for them to serve in a foreign army. The French also had their restrictions on

Fig 1. The Indian Head
squadron insignia that was
painted on the fuselages of
all the Escadrille planes

foreign volunteers. Foreigners could become ambulance
drivers, something considered to be a noncombatant occupation, or they could enlist in the French Foreign Legion,
whose members took an oath of allegiance to the Legion,
and not to France.

When French military aviation eventually began to
accept American pilots, those men initially flew as individuals with French squadrons, but in time an all-American
squadron known as the Lafayette Escadrille—French for
"squadron"—came into being. They wore French uniforms
and were part of the French Army, and the dramatic part
they played brought them instant fame. Men on both sides
who shot down five or more enemy planes were known as
"aces," and invariably received decorations for valor.

This book is the Escadrille's story, an account of what
one of its surviving American volunteer pilots later called
"the startling success of that intrepid band." It is not a history of the First World War, nor a comprehensive account
of that war's aerial battles. It is not a linear history that
records events in the order they occurred. This is more
of a mosaic, an emotional portrait, a testament to human
courage and ingenuity.

One

By God I Know Mighty Well
What I Would Do!

In the summer of 1914 numbers of young American men were in Paris, or doing such things as hiking in the Alps. When the news came that Germany had declared war on France, on August 3rd other young Americans boarded ships in East Coast ports and headed across the Atlantic. Two days after the war began a group of those already in Paris who wanted to fight for France went to the American Embassy and requested a meeting with Ambassador Myron T. Herrick. They knew that under President Woodrow Wilson the United States had adopted an official position of neutrality, and they needed to discuss their status.

    Herrick was sixty years old, a farmer's son from Ohio who, at the age of nineteen, had taught in a one-room schoolhouse earning money to go to Oberlin College and serve as the Governor of Ohio before accepting the Ambassadorship to France. Years later he recorded what happened at that meeting.

"They filed into my office . . . They wanted to enlist in the French Army. There were no protestations, no speeches; they merely wanted to fight, and they asked me if they had a right to do so, if it was legal.

"That moment remains impressed in my memory as though it had happened yesterday; it was one of the most trying in my whole official experience. I wanted to take those boys to my heart and cry, 'God bless you! Go!' But I was held back from doing so by the fact that I was an ambassador. But I loved them, every one, as though they were my own.

"I got out the law on the duties of neutrals; I read it to them and explained its passages. I really tried not to do more, but it was no use. Those young eyes were searching mine, seeking, I am sure, the encouragement they had come in hope of getting.

"It was more than flesh and blood could stand, and catching fire myself from their eagerness, I brought down my fist on the table saying, 'That is the law, boys; but if I was young and in your shoes, by God I know mighty well what I would do!'

"At this they set up a regular shout, each gripped me by the hand, and then they went rushing down the stairs . . . They all proceeded straight to the Rue de Grenelle and took service in the Foreign Legion."

These young Americans knew that by enlisting in the Foreign Legion they might be endangering their American citizenship, but they went ahead. In his autobiography Herrick said this:

"I think the people of the United States owe a very special debt to these boys and to those who afterward created the Lafayette Escadrille. During three terrible, long years [between 1914 and 1917] when the sting of criticism [for not entering the war] cut into every American soul, they were showing the world how their countrymen could fight if only they were allowed the opportunity. To many of us they seemed the saviors of our national honor, giving the lie to current sneers upon the courage of our nation.

"Their influence upon sentiment at home was also tremendous . . . Here were Americans shedding their blood for a cause in which America's heart was also engaged and to which later she pledged the lives . . . of her sons. I suppose that without them we would doubtless have entered the war, but the shout they sent up as they left my office was answered by millions of passionate voices urging the authorities of their government to act. Nothing is more just than that these first defenders of our country's good name should be singled out for special love and reverence by ourselves, just as they have been by the French."

Herrick took the position held by many Americans, but a balanced account of the views of the American public at the time would include strong isolationist sentiments. While former president Theodore Roosevelt and other prominent figures believed that the United States should enter the war, many millions of Americans saw no reason to become involved in an increasingly bloody struggle among European powers. Tremendous numbers of descendants of German immigrants did not want to fight the land of their ancestors, and equal numbers of Irish-Americans saw England as the nation that had oppressed and exploited Ireland for centuries.

Nonetheless, France was at war, and many young Americans felt moved to come to her aid. One who had lived in Paris and would fly with the Escadrille wrote, "We weren't fooled into thinking that the World War was entirely a thing invented by the Boche [Germans], but there was no getting around the fact that the Boche had been looking for a chance to start something, and now that the chance came, we Americans who had enjoyed the hospitality of France and had learned to love the country and the people, simply had to fight. Our consciences demanded it."

As for the men in the American expatriate colony in Paris who were above military age, many of them and their

Fig 2. This photo in the *Paris Herald* (later the *Paris Herald Tribune*) of August 26, 1914, shows the first group of American volunteers to fight for France marching through Paris to a train station from which they will go to a French Army base in Rouen.

wives also felt passionately attached to the French cause. They threw themselves into activities such as volunteer work at the American Hospital in the large Paris suburb of Neuilly. The hospital, built by the same expat American surgeon who played a role in the founding of the Lafayette Escadrille, cared for many American casualties before the United States entered the war.

Two

How the New Thing Grew

When the Germans declared war on France in 1914, only eleven years had passed since the Wright brothers made their first flights near Kitty Hawk. The war brought about a major acceleration in the development of everything about aircraft—the materials used; the shape, design, and strength of the wings and tail; the controls; the engines. Nonetheless, initially they remained largely made of canvas and wood, held together by metal components such as metal pipes and baling wire. An Escadrille pilot wrote, "With only slight exaggeration, it seemed as if they were merely gathered-up odds and ends of wood, discarded matchsticks, and the like, which were wired together, catch-as-catch-can fashion . . . Then old handkerchiefs were sewed together to cover the wings and that part of the fuselage around the pilot's seat. The remainder of the fuselage was left naked, which gave the plane a sort of half-finished appearance." The fighter planes looked sleek and graceful, compared with the bombers. One flier said of a type of bomber called a Voisin, "They looked like flying baby carriages." Fighter pilots called the bomber pilots "truck drivers."

As the war progressed, more and more parts of the planes were manufactured from metal, but bullets could always cut through any steel fuselage. Each wartime year, the Germans brought out an improved plane, only to have the Allies put a better one into production a few months later. One of the best Allied fighters, the SPAD, had a flipped-off-the-tongue English-sounding name, but it was the acronym for *Société Pour L'Aviation et ses Dérivés* (Society for Aviation and Its Derivatives), a French corporation started not by an engineer but by Armand Deperdussin, a traveling salesman and cabaret singer who first made a fortune in the silk business. The Germans received enormous help from a young Dutchman named Anthony Fokker, who not only designed first-rate aircraft and built them, but also devised the "Interrupter Mechanism," which synchronized machine guns mounted behind a plane's propeller so that they fired with the bullets passing between the spinning blades, rather than hitting them. Until the Interrupter Mechanism evolved, pilots of single-seat fighters had to stand up behind the controls and awkwardly bring into play a machine gun such as a Lewis gun, mounted on a pivot that swung in a limited arc either on one side of the cockpit or above it. In a two-seater plane, the man in the backseat faced to the rear, holding a machine gun that had a much larger field of fire. (The rear-facing gunner, who could fire off to either side as well, posed such a threat that the French even introduced a plane that had a dummy holding a machine gun that was placed in the rear seat.)

In the larger sense, this evolution of the airplane continued the technical competition that warfare always stimulates. Inventions and improvements: the stirrup; the crossbow; stronger steel for breastplates, helmets, and swords. Gunpowder: the rifle, producing greater distance and accuracy than the musket; the revolver, firing faster than the flintlock pistol; the revolutionary and dreadfully lethal machine gun. And now, the possibilities of what the airplane could do.

France's Marshal Ferdinand Foch said in 1910, seven years after Kitty Hawk, "The airplane is all very well for sport, but useless for the army." He underestimated the speed with which aeronautical and political history were moving. In Europe, as in America, what this new "flying machine"—pilots later referred to their planes as "my machine" —could do fascinated the public. Crowds numbering tens of thousands attended air shows at which barnstorming pilots performed thrilling maneuvers and aviators competed for large cash prizes in air races.

As for the airplane being "useless for the army," when what became known as The Great War broke out in 1914, these flimsy contraptions had advanced to the point that they were regarded as a piece of military equipment like a pair of binoculars, useful in observing and photographing enemy positions and movements. In the war's first months, pilots of both sides would pass each other in their planes, heading out to observe the enemy on the ground like commuters going to work. Some of the opposing pilots even gave each other friendly waves.

Soon, the ability to see the enemy on the ground from the air started to produce spectacular results. A month after the war began, two large German armies were only thirty miles from Paris, advancing swiftly toward the Marne River. On September 6, French observation planes reported seeing a gap between the two enormous phalanxes. In the most dramatic action of the war, thousands of commandeered Paris taxicabs and buses rushed reinforcements to the front, just in time to prevent the two German armies from consolidating their attack. In the "Miracle of the Marne," the Allied counterattack slammed into the gap and pushed the Germans back forty miles. That saved Paris—and if the capital of France had fallen, such a strategic and psychological defeat might have led to early German victory. A total of two million French and German soldiers fought in the battle—the largest in history to that time—and more than a hundred thousand were killed or wounded.

Although few realized it then, the early battles of the war marked out an area running from the North Sea to the mountainous Swiss border that became known as the Western Front. During the next four years, thirteen million men would be killed, wounded, captured, or become missing in the trench warfare that took place in that territory. When the Lafayette Escadrille was formed, it would eventually be stationed at nine different airfields behind those bloody lines. As for making aerial photographs of enemy positions, French observation planes soon began taking thousands of pictures a day.

The airplane had indeed become an integral part of the immense struggle. Both sides came to recognize the effectiveness of aerial observation; fighter planes, also known as "pursuit" aircraft, began to be sent on individual missions whose purpose was to shoot down the enemy's observation planes. These developed into missions such as the famous "dawn patrols," in which several of a fighter squadron's planes would go out in formation, looking for any type of enemy planes to shoot down. When they encountered similar enemy formations, the legendary "dog-fights" would occur.

Well prior to the war, the term "dogfight" signified a violent struggle, usually between two opponents. Applied to the new war in the air, it usually referred to a situation in which, when several planes from one side encountered those from the other, the combat broke up into pairs of planes fighting aerial duels.

The war's greatest master of the dogfight proved to be a twenty-four-year-old German pilot, Baron Manfred von Richthofen, known as the "Red Baron" because of the blood-red color of his three-winged Fokker fighter plane. Victor in eighty combats in which the pilot who was shot down was often called a "kill," he wrote an account of one of his most famous fights. Although Richthofen did not know it, his opponent was the noted British pilot Major Lance Hawker, whose exploits had won him the Victoria Cross, Britain's highest medal for valor.

"One day," Richthofen wrote, "I was blithely fly-ing . . . when I noticed three Englishmen who also had apparently gone a-hunting. I noticed that they were ogling me and as I felt much inclination to fight I did not want to disappoint them.

Fig 3. Baron Manfred von Richthofen, the German fighter pilot who was the war's leading ace, with eighty Allied planes shot down. He started the war as a cavalry officer and always referred to Captain Oswald Boelcke as his flying instructor. Finally killed six months before the war's end, he was given a full military funeral with every honor by the British and Australian troops in whose territory he crashed.

"I was flying at a lower altitude. Consequently I had to wait until one of my English friends tried to drop on me. After a while one of the three came sailing along and attempted to tackle me in the rear. After firing five shots he had to stop because I had swerved in a sharp curve.

"The Englishman tried to catch me up in the rear while I tried to get behind him. So we circled round and round like madmen after one another at an altitude of about 10,000 feet.

"First we circled twenty times to the left, and then thirty times to the right. Each tried to get behind and above the other. Soon I discovered that I was not meeting a beginner. He had not the slightest intention of breaking off the fight. He was traveling in a machine which turned beautifully. However, my own was better at rising than his, and I succeeded at last in getting above and behind my English waltzing partner.

"When we had got down to about 6,000 feet without achieving anything in particular, my opponent ought to have discovered that it was time for him to take his leave. The wind was favorable to me for it drove us more and more to the German position. At last we were above Bapaume, about half a mile behind the German front. The impertinent fellow was full of cheek and when we got down to about 3,000 feet he merrily waved to me as if to say, 'Well, how do you do?'

"The circles which we made around each other were so narrow that their diameter was probably no more than 250 or 300 feet. I had time to take a good look at my opponent. I looked down into his carriage [cockpit] and could see every movement of his head. If he had not had his cap on I would have noticed what kind of a face he was making.

"My Englishman was a good sportsman, but by and by the flying got a little too hot for him. He had to decide whether he would land on German ground or whether he would fly back to the English lines. Of course he tried the latter, after having endeavored in vain to escape me by loopings and such like tricks. At that time his first bullets were flying around me, for hitherto neither of us had been able to do any shooting.

"When he had come down to about 300 feet he tried to escape by flying in a zig-zag course. That was my most favorable moment. I followed him at an altitude of 250 feet to 150 feet, firing all the time. The Englishman could not help falling. But the jamming of my gun nearly robbed me of my success.

"My opponent fell, shot through the head, 150 feet behind our line. His machine gun was dug out of the ground and it ornaments the entrance of my dwelling."

Richthofen knew himself, and wrote this:

"My father discriminates between being a sportsman and a butcher. When I have shot down an Englishman my hunting passion is satisfied for a quarter of an hour. Therefore I do not succeed in shooting down two Englishmen in succession. If one of them comes down I have the feeling of complete satisfaction. Only much, much later I have overcome my instincts and become a butcher."

Three

Aspects of the Great
New Dimension

From the Wright brothers' flights near Kitty Hawk in 1903 to Hiroshima in 1945, aviation redefined the known world.

Early in those forty-two years, the First World War brought about warfare on a previously unknown scale, and assimilated into the struggle a new factor—human beings could fly.

Kitty Hawk was the birth of aviation, and World War One can be called its violent adolescence. The Americans of the Lafayette Escadrille flew in France in French planes and wore French uniforms, but their exploits marked the first time American pilots flew together as a unit in aerial warfare.

Aviation has been a tremendous historical development. For eons, all human activity moved in a way measured by length and breadth, with heights no greater than mountaintops and depths reaching not far below the surface of land or sea. Then it suddenly became possible for men and women to fly immensely higher and faster and farther than the birds they had always watched. Balloons and gliders created interest, but powered flight is one of the supremely important inventions: It is perhaps the most transformational engineering feat of all time, and has proven to be as important as the creation of the wheel, the invention of inoculation, and the harnessing of steam and electricity. In terms of war, this "air arm" meant that an army could put fast-moving eyes into the sky many miles from its ground forces, and drop explosives far beyond the previous range of the most powerful cannons. In effect, a new kind of front line could be established, high in the sky.

As the war developed, many Allied fighter planes, including those of the Lafayette Escadrille, protected Allied bombers as they flew over enemy territory. A notable mission in which pilots of the Escadrille participated occurred on October 12, 1916. Allied bombs destroyed parts of the important German Mauser rifle factory at Oberndorf, which shipped twenty thousand rifles a day to the front. Air power's potential was there for all to see.

Early in the war, French intelligence officers began to realize that, in addition to attacking German aircraft and observing enemy movements and positions from the air, planes could be used to place spies miles behind enemy lines. This led to a daring aerial exploit, involving a twenty-nine-year-old American volunteer named Jules James Bach, from New Orleans. He received his education in England and France, being granted a degree in mechanical engineering from the

Sorbonne in Paris in 1904 and a degree in civil engineering from the *École Centrale* in Paris in 1908. Bach understood the workings of the primitive gasoline engines of the day, as well as the developing science of aerodynamics.

When the war erupted in 1914, Bach wanted to fight for France. "Jimmy," as his comrades called him, became one of the first Americans to join the Legion, as a poilu: a foot soldier.

During his four months in the trenches, Bach experienced what was later described by another American who endured similar danger and privation:

"He was one of that famed band of Legionnaires who made the historic march, under full equipment, of fifty-six kilometers [thirty-four miles], from Verzenay to Fismes; the longest, most grueling march made by any soldiers in the World War. From four in the morning till eleven at night, with only a cup of bitter black coffee to sustain them, they marched without food, practically without a halt, except for the ten-minute rest period each hour.

"It was a killing test for men fresh from civilian life. The last few hours were so sodden in misery that the men staggered on automatically in a sort of a daze. When a halt was called, they threw themselves down and slept on rock piles or anything at hand to keep them out of the mud . . . Gradually becoming immune to such hardships, Jimmy went through all the stiffest engagements and hand-to-hand fighting with hardly a scratch."

In December of that first year of the war, long before the Lafayette Escadrille was created, Bach was accepted into the French Army's *Service Aeronautique*. After training in French aviation schools for five months, he received his brevet, the designation of being a pilot, and flew reconnaissance missions for a month at the front, wearing a French uniform indicating his rank of corporal and flying with a French squadron.

Then Bach and a French sergeant-pilot named Mangeot were given a particularly dangerous assignment, to take place on September 23, 1915, before the great majority of American pilots saw action. Using their two-seater observation planes, they were to land at first light behind enemy lines, swiftly drop off two French soldiers who were wearing civilian clothes and acting as spies, and leave as quickly as they had come. The two spies, who knew the territory where they were to operate, carried explosives: Their mission was to blow up a strategic stretch of enemy-held railroad track miles from where they landed, make notes on enemy positions in that area, and attempt to get back on foot through the opposing German and French lines.

All four men knew the risks involved. If the two spies in civilian clothes were captured, they would be shot. If either Bach or Mangeot were captured and found to be connected with the spies, they too would almost certainly be executed, even though they wore French uniforms.

The two planes landed in a remote but poorly chosen field, covered with bushes and saplings. Bach and Mangeot made skillful landings; each spy clambered out of the plane in which he had been a passenger, holding his armful of explosives, and began the hike that would take him to the railroad track.

Bach took off immediately, but as he looked back he saw that Mangeot's plane, taking off just behind him, had struck some object and was lying upside down on the rough ground. Bach turned and landed next to the wrecked plane. Mangeot was able to crawl from beneath it, dash toward him, and jump into the rear seat behind Bach. As Bach started to take off a second time, one of his wings caught on the limb of a tree, and it crashed. Both men were unhurt, and realized that the longer they could remain hidden in the thick nearby woods, giving the two spies time to get farther from them, the less chance there was that, if any of the four of them were captured, the Germans would recognize that they were all participants in the same mission.

Bach and Mangeot remained hidden all through the day. By evening they felt certain that the spies were miles from them. Then they started off in their quest to get through the opposing lines of trenches and return safely to their base. After a few hours they were captured and taken to the small city of Laon, where they were questioned by German intelligence officers. It was then that they discovered that the railroad track had indeed been blown up. Their inquisitors decided that Bach and Mangeot, who admitted that the planes were theirs but refused to answer further questions, were prime suspects in an act of espionage. Instead of receiving the routine treatment of being sent off to a camp for prisoners of war, Bach and Mangeot were put on trial.

In the first trial, the prosecutor, a German officer, was determined to have Bach receive the maximum sentence. Bach was an American, and fell into the category of being a *franc-tireur*—a mercenary fighting in the uniform of an enemy of Germany. Under German law, that was enough for him to be executed for the crime of espionage. Although the prosecutor treated Bach as his prize defendant, he also asked that Mangeot be shot.

Fully aware that this was truly a do-or-die situation, Bach received the court's permission to conduct his own defense. He pleaded his and Mangeot's case with eloquence, insisting that there was insufficient evidence to prove that he and Mangeot were guilty of espionage. The court agreed that Bach should have a second trial, ten days after the first. He would have ten days to produce favorable evidence.

This placed the two defendants in an agonizing situation. While Bach might come up with evidence helpful to his and Mangeot's case, on any one of those ten more days the two spies who had blown up the track might be captured, and the fate of all four men would be sealed.

What happened next involved an apparent intrigue. Although behind bars, Bach somehow had access to significant funds. He received the court's permission to hire one of Germany's most gifted trial lawyers. The man arrived from Berlin, doubting that he could save his clients' lives. What may have gone on behind the scenes has never emerged, but when the court reconvened the two spies were still at large, and there was no additional incriminating evidence. According to one account, "The Berlin lawyer threw himself heart and soul into the defense of his clients," using "brilliant and impassioned oratory."

The decisive hour came, and Jimmy Bach and Mangeot rose to learn their fate. "By the unanimous verdict of this court," the judge-advocate told them, "the French aviators

Bach and Mangeot, accused of espionage, are found not guilty. It is directed that they be held and confined as honorable prisoners of war."

After some days of continued confinement in the prison at Laon, the two men began planning an escape. On the day they intended to make the escape, Jimmy Bach was sent to a military prison in Bavaria, much farther from French territory. It was an old castle on a mountaintop, with sheer cliffs on three sides. Despite the near-impossibility of escaping, one evening Bach succeeded. He made his way through the darkness to the house of a woman who his fellow prisoners had told him was a French sympathizer. She was from Alsace-Lorraine, and her house was one of a chain of places that had been set up early in the war to aid escaping prisoners.

The woman welcomed him in from the night and sheltered him until morning, when he planned to go on his way. But as he started to leave, a squad of German soldiers who had been keeping the house under surveillance surrounded him. Before being marched back to the hilltop prison, Bach was forced to watch the woman being shot.

By now Jimmy Bach was a marked man, and was transported under heavy guard to Germany's most formidable prison, the central fortress at Nuremberg. He made several attempts to escape and never succeeded; nor did any other prisoner held there. Jimmy Bach was the Germans' first American prisoner of war, and because they enjoyed inventing and bestowing titles of all kinds, by seniority he was named the Herr Direktor of the Amerikanischer-Kriegsgefangenen Club, the association of American prisoners of war.

Four

What Manner of Men?

Who were these young Americans who began flying above the bloody battlefields of France? Their photographs tell the story. Sharp clear eyes look out of healthy faces. The expressions are confident. Many of these men played football, hockey, polo—sports that required courage, endurance, and superior reflexes. A few were race car drivers. Others were gifted in fields as varied as architecture, music, painting, electronics, and writing. Many proved themselves capable of putting forth remarkable mental and physical energy.

These young warriors were indeed individualistic, but even before the war, Americans of every sort sensed that with the airplane, something tremendously forceful and challenging had come to them. An immensely vigorous young nation, seeking its identity, consumed by its industrialization and just coming onto the world stage, saw an expansion of its destiny in the skies. Less than ten years after

Kitty Hawk, America had become aware of an enormous event on the horizon, an impending European war certain to eclipse all previous military struggles.

This prospect of a huge looming conflict, offering battle in a new dimension, presented challenges to different instincts. For many high-spirited, energetic young Americans, an inner voice said, *"I need to meet what is coming. I need to equal, defend against, and if necessary defeat those who can use this new force against me and mine."*

Were these instincts clothed in idealism? How to view these pilots of the Escadrille? Were they adventurers, or patriots scouting out this new territory? Were they scientists of a sort, participating in a huge experiment? Their sincerely stated beliefs and purpose could have been one thing, but the force driving them might well have been a form of collective survival instinct.

The thirty-eight pilots who originally composed the Lafayette Escadrille represented all of this. They were actors in an epic drama—a mere handful of men, most of them crossing an ocean to fight for a foreign land in an unprecedented venture. History offers few such examples. Theirs is the encompassing story; theirs is a revealing drama of that era. They experienced it all—valor, terror, cowardice, instinctive skill, love of comrades, colorful appeal to women, fatal decisions made when split-second actions determined whether a pilot lived or died.

The war killed many of them. Some of the survivors went on to be richly rewarded pioneers in peacetime aviation. Others became leaders in the armies of the air that clashed in the skies and destroyed cities in the larger war that came twenty years later. Just as this first air war made some of them formidable men, it broke others. There were suicides, then and later, and those who hollowed themselves out with alcohol and other drugs.

Every form of these behaviors, every result, was to be found in the Lafayette Escadrille, and in their reactions to the far-better-organized, better-trained, greatly experienced German pilots they opposed. Pilot after pilot became the Everyman of the skies. They wrote letters, they kept diaries, they wrote books, they had mothers, fathers, brothers, sisters, loving women who grieved over their deaths. Some wounded men met French nurses in frontline hospitals. After the war four brave French nurses married their patients. Three of the surviving fliers went on to marry movie stars.

At their flying fields behind the trenches these young men—their average age was twenty-four—kept pets, mostly dogs. In time the menagerie grew to include two fast-growing lion cubs, an Irish terrier that accompanied its master on low-flying missions, and a skunk that had been altered so it could not spray its scent. To immerse oneself in the Lafayette experience is to enter a huge human story that can be viewed through one blood-spattered window.

In all, 269 American pilots flew with various French squadrons before the United States entered the war. They were listed as being in the Lafayette Flying Corps, but the Lafayette Escadrille was the only squadron that, with the exception of its French commander Captain Georges Thenault and two attached French lieutenants, was composed entirely of Americans. Of those thirty-eight young volunteers, men from twelve states, eleven were destined to die.

Among the total of 269 American pilots who flew for the French, including those in the Escadrille, forty-two were killed in action or received fatal wounds, twenty-one died in accidents, four died of illness, and two committed suicide. This meant that of those who volunteered, one out of four died; and more than that sustained nonlethal wounds.

They flew in flimsy contraptions with faulty engines and machine guns that frequently jammed and stopped firing. It took a special kind of bravery to face, on every takeoff, a known, serious risk of early death. Perhaps it involved an almost unperceived awareness of life's ironies, and a touch of bravado that concealed a very mortal, ultimate need for, above all else, some love. Pilot Ned Parsons, a handsome twenty-four-year-old from Springfield, Massachusetts, described a throwback to knights in armor going into battle with their ladies' scarves or long gloves tied around their arms. In this case the amulet was a woman's stocking, worn under a soft leather flying helmet.

"The top fitted over the skull, while the leg and foot went under the chin and was tucked up on the other side. It was useful in keeping our heads warm as well as being a strong charm. Not any silk stocking would do. It had to be a stocking from some girl you loved or vice versa, and had to be well worn. If anything happened to you while wearing it, it was a sure sign the girl didn't love you any more or never had. The personality that the stocking assumed through having been worn was held sufficient to keep you out of trouble."

This idea of amulets extended into different forms of superstition. Ned Parsons said, "War aviators individually and collectively were the most superstitious beings in the world," and offered some examples from his own experience. Many pilots began to collect small metal objects, including religious medals, that they strung around their wrists like charm bracelets. Parsons observed, "Usually a man's length of service could be approximated by the number of medals he had jangling on his wrist. Some of the old-timers had to wear chains on each wrist to hold them."

He spoke of his own particularly special experience:

"But the most prized of all talismans for me was my black cat. Black cats are popularly supposed to be anathema, but mine must have been a different breed of cat.

"For five months, I fought Huns all over the sky . . . But I could never get one to fall. Then I had the good fortune to meet a beautiful Parisienne named Renee de Ranville . . . Renee bought me one of those big, life-sized velvet cats with arched back, tail standing up, and a look of almost human intelligence on the whiskered face."

Parsons had his mechanic Henriot wire the cat statue to the center strut of his right wing. "From then on, it rode with me from the Channel to the Vosges. Whiskers streaming back in the slipstream, he or she (I never could decide) kept an eye on everything. It always gave me a lot of courage in a tight place to see the very placid expression on her or his face. If the cat wasn't worried, why should I be?"

Parsons' luck changed, and he brought down his first enemy plane. The critical moment came, however, when he managed to maneuver out of a desperate situation in which three German fighters surrounded him, with many bullets striking his plane. "I was plenty scared with my narrow escape and . . . hurried back to the field . . . just in time! My whole tail assembly was torn to pieces, and two of the wires controlling my elevator were hanging by just one strand. Here and there was a hole in the wings or fuselage, but I discovered no other damage until I happened to look at the cat. Sawdust was dripping out of a ragged hole in her side. Somewhere deep in the black cat's vitals was a German slug with my name engraved on it! Since it didn't go through, the bullet must have been nearly spent when it hit, but in lining it up from the direction it entered I found that, if the cat hadn't been there, it would in all probability have punctured my eardrum. We performed a surgical operation with needle and thread." Parsons said of the cat, "It flew with me as long as I was with the Lafayette Escadrille . . . and continued to exercise a benign influence to the end of the war."

Other than superstitions, this new war in the air developed its own culture, its own courtesies and customs. One pilot wrote that these included things such as "a salute or wave of the hand to some adversary when the duel had been called a draw [when both pilots were out of ammunition or fuel]; or letters passed back and forth, dropped over the lines, inquiring about the fate of a comrade or expressing regret for the death of some gallant enemy pilot, which rarely failed to bring an answer; or a wreath dropped during the funeral ceremonies of some well-known ace."

When the Germans shot down an Allied plane, if the pilot's physical condition permitted it he was taken to the officers' mess hall of the squadron whose prisoner he had become. There he received its hospitality, including an elaborate meal and a standing toast to his valor, before being sent off in a staff car to a prisoner-of-war camp. German pilots who fell into Allied hands received the same treatment.

Soon after the first Escadrille pilots reached the front, they became part of another tradition, begun by Paul Rockwell from North Carolina, who with his younger brother Kiffin had enlisted in the French Foreign Legion in August of 1914. Three months later Paul was severely wounded when a German shell exploded next to where he stood outside a trench, flinging him into the trench and shattering his collarbone. The doctors determined that he would never fully regain his strength or range of motion, and he received an honorable discharge. He then started working in Paris as an official civilian combat correspondent with the *Section d'Information* of the French Ministry of Public Information, operating out of French Army headquarters in Paris. He also gathered stories about the war for the *Chicago Daily News.*

Paul's brother Kiffin was able to transfer into French aviation, and when he shot down the first of the Escadrille's "kills," Paul hurried from Paris to Luxeuil, an airfield near the Swiss border where the Escadrille was stationed, carrying "a rare and precious bottle of very old bourbon." Kiffin opened the bottle, intending that everyone should have a drink. Then the suggestion was made that Kiffin should take a pull from it, after which the bottle should be corked and not opened again until another pilot should make a kill and have a pull, and from then on "every man who brings down a German is entitled to one good slug."

Figs 4 and 5. Kiffin Yates Rockwell was one of the "Founders," the term by which the first seven pilots who joined the Lafayette Escadrille were known. Rockwell was from Asheville, North Carolina, and studied for a time at Washington and Lee University in Lexington, Virginia. In the picture on the left, he is the man to the left of the tree, fighting as an infantryman in the French Foreign Legion before becoming a pilot in the Escadrille, the uniform of which he is wearing in the picture on the right. Wounded both in ground fighting and in the air, Rockwell was killed in action in a "dogfight" three days after his twenty-fourth birthday. A fellow pilot described him as "brave to the core, never flinching."

Twenty-one years later, Ned Parsons wrote this:

"When the ceremony was started, no one had any idea that the bottle would outlive the Escadrille, but such was the startling success of that intrepid band that the contents were soon exhausted. It was never replaced, but the empty bottle was faithfully guarded by Billy Thaw, our [unofficial

American] commanding officer, and only came to light again when he died recently. It became known in Escadrille lore as 'The Bottle of Death.'"

One practice, in a sense symbolized by that bottle, was the serious business of confirming a kill. Many aerial duels ended with a damaged plane disappearing behind enemy lines. The squadrons on both sides wanted to know whether the enemy plane had been shot down by one of their pilots, or by antiaircraft fire, or had experienced engine failure. The rule became that for it to be considered a kill, at least two qualified men, either in the air or on the ground, had to see the plane hit the ground, or, for example, see it go down in flames behind trees, followed by an immediate explosion.

In trying to establish what had in fact happened, men from a squadron, pilots or intelligence officers, constantly risked their lives by going to forward trenches. Sometimes they could see the wreckage of their own or enemy aircraft, or talk with foot soldiers who'd seen the results of dogfights taking place above their heads. It became a grim sort of keeping score; for an individual pilot to shoot down five planes meant that he became an "ace." This recognition usually brought with it medals, promotions, and cash rewards. For the intelligence officers, analysis of the performance of different Allied squadrons, or of opposing enemy squadrons, might dictate the need to change the lineup along a sector of the front.

Destined to be pilots or not, these spirited American volunteers were good-looking, virile, and heroes of the hour. The young Frenchwomen were crazy about them.

When the American recruits first went off to training camps from Paris, one of them wrote this account of what happened at the railroad station.

"At the Gare St. Lazare our little detachment was causing a tremendous excitement. The waiting rooms, the entrance to the platforms and the platforms themselves were crowded with bon voyage parties. At least seven ladies for every member of the American Volunteer Corps had put in an appearance. Each one of them thought she was the only one. There were several unfortunate occurrences. There is a legend about what happened after the train pulled out—a legend about hair pulling and other forms of female combativeness."

Five

Contrasts

Before the pilots of the Escadrille flew from their base at Bar-le-Duc, 130 miles northeast of Paris, the "Founders," as the first of them became known, were stationed for a month at Luxeuil, the largest and most picturesque airfield in France. It covered a flat grassy expanse two miles long, surrounded by high slopes in the foothills of the Vosges Mountains near the Swiss border. In that militarily quiet area, they received their training in formation flying.

Luxeuil entered history as a campground for the Roman legions, whose warriors were attracted to it by the hot springs bubbling out of the ground. It eventually became an exclusive spa, a small resort favored by French royalty such as King Louis XV and his Polish queen, Marie.

The American pilots, several of whose introductions to the war had come during the early brutal battles fought by the Foreign Legion, lived in a stone villa next to the ancient Roman baths. Each man had a room of his own, complete

with a feather bed and a window offering a view of the large
nearby hills. They took their meals at the Hotel Pomme
d'Or, just down the street, where the linen tablecloths were
loaded with such delicacies as roasted grouse and baked rab-
bit, which the pilots washed down with vintage Burgundy
followed by "individual aluminum pots of filtered coffee."
In the handsomely appointed clubroom they shared in the
villa, a phonograph played such currently popular records
as "Don't Go Away," "Keep the Home Fires Burning," and
the lilting "It's a Long Way to Tipperary."

Kiffin Rockwell, brother of Paul Rockwell, who had
been wounded fighting in the Foreign Legion and was now
an official combat correspondent, had also been wounded
in action with the Foreign Legion. He had recovered from
his wounds and now flew for the Escadrille. Kiffin wrote his
mother this: "We all eat together at a hotel where wonderful meals are served . . . We go down each day about 100
yards from here to bathe in a bath-house that is 200 years
old. The scenery around the town is wonderful . . . [we] are
planning a little fishing and hunting, so you can see that it is
not much like being at war." He later added this thought: "I
am sitting by my window now with a good warm sun coming in and a wonderful view of the birds singing. If it were
not for looking in the glass and seeing myself in uniform I
should not be able to believe that I am at war, or that there
is such a thing as war."

That changed. Two days before the squadron was to
leave for far more active missions at Bar-le-Duc, Kiffin was
flying back toward Luxeuil from a patrol during which he
encountered no German planes. Suddenly he saw an enemy

two-seater two thousand feet below him. Diving at it, he felt his plane shake as a burst of machine gun fire struck it, but he had this reaction: "I didn't pay any attention to that and kept going straight for him, until I got within 25 or 30 meters of him." Opening fire and cutting away just in time to avoid a collision, he saw "black, greasy smoke" start to pour from the two-seater as it began a dive in which it took three minutes to plummet to the ground and explode in flames.

A front-line French observation post immediately telephoned in a confirmation of Kiffin's "victory." By the time he landed at Luxeuil, he found his squadron mates standing out on the grassy airstrip, waiting to lift him out of his plane and carry him into squadron headquarters on their shoulders to be debriefed. His friend Jim McConnell said, "All Luxeuil smiled upon him—particularly the girls." Another pilot recalled that "Kiffin was a popular hero—the girls gave him bunches of flowers and the hotel-keepers sent him bottles of champagne." Although individual members of the Escadrille had made kills while flying with French squadrons, this was the first enemy plane shot down by the Lafayette Escadrille after it was officially organized. That news was telephoned to Paris, where it produced "a tremendous wave of excitement."

To bring the Lafayette Escadrille into being required both money and influence. Later it appeared that early in the war a number of individuals had started to think about having at least one French aviation unit consist exclusively of American pilots, but credit for making the first moves to accomplish that belonged in good part to the American surgeon Dr. Edmund Gros. He had moved to Paris from San Francisco before the war, and was one of the prominent members of the expatriate community, many of whom became his patients. With the help of rich American residents of Paris such as Mr. and Mrs. William K. Vanderbilt, he had built the American Hospital, and with the start of the war he was one of those who established the American Ambulance Service, soon renamed the American Field Service.

As that organization began to move under its own management, Dr. Gros felt free to begin pushing for a specific American role in the rapidly developing air war. He called on his friends the Vanderbilts in their mansion, told them about his hope to create an all-American squadron, and added that he thought it would require some money to make it a reality.

According to Dr. Gros, as soon as he finished speaking, Mrs. Vanderbilt, whose maiden name was Harriman and who had her own fortune from that family's railroad empire, "walked to her desk and wrote out a check for five thousand dollars." Then she looked at her husband and said, "Now, 'K,' what will you do?" He wrote out a check for fifteen thousand dollars, and followed that with other large sums throughout the war. Among other things, the money was used to augment the American fliers' very low French Army pay and to give pilots cash prizes for successful missions.

Encouraged by the Vanderbilts' support, Dr. Gros turned to other allies. One of the first to come to his side was twenty-nine-year-old Bill Thaw. In these first years of the war, no other American pilot displayed such a combination of flying skill and leadership ability. His prewar interest in flying had brought him into contact with the American inventors, designers, and manufacturers who quickly became attracted to aviation. A rich young man and a cousin of Harry Thaw, who shot the famous architect Stanford White in one of the most sensational jealousy murders of the early twentieth century, Bill Thaw was the son of a prominent manufacturing family in Pittsburgh. He was a sophomore in good standing at Yale, but his interest in flying consumed him to the point that his father agreed that he should withdraw from the university and take lessons at a flying school at Hammondsport, New York, run by Glenn Curtiss, a leader in the creation of the American aviation industry.

Young Bill Thaw excelled at Curtiss's flying school, and his father bought him one of the Model E Hydro two-seater flying boats that Curtiss was building. Thaw's own flying career took off. At an air race in Manhattan, he saved time by flying his seaplane under the four bridges then leading out of the city, something never done before, and later took a paying passenger on a flight in which he circled the Statue of Liberty twice, closely passing the metal torch at a distance of two hundred feet. He also made one of the first shore-to-ship deliveries when he dropped a bundle of local newspapers onto the deck of the German ship *Imperator* as she steamed into New York harbor.

Two years before the war, Bill Thaw moved to France. When war broke out in August of 1914, he was taking

Fig 6. William Thaw, from a prominent family in Pittsburgh, holding the squadron's lion mascot "Whiskey" when he was a cub. A natural leader who was the de facto American commander of the Escadrille, Thaw was an accomplished prewar flier in the United States. During an air race, he flew under the four bridges leading out of New York City, an unprecedented feat.

paying passengers for flights in a seaplane along the red cliffs and brilliant beaches of the French Riviera. Thaw gave his plane to the French government and enlisted in the Foreign Legion. An American friend described him as "a burly brute with a splendid physique, thick black hair, snapping black eyes, and a pair of flowing mustachios that were the pride of his heart. When they were waxed, Bill looked every inch the dapper officer, but when, as more often happened, they drooped, Bill had the benign air of a venerable walrus."

On a day in October of 1914 when Thaw and some other Americans were in a trench near Verzenay, a small town a hundred miles northeast of Paris near Rheims, he saw a German plane overhead and told his comrades, "One

day, a squadron of Americans will be flying for France."
Eager to get back in the air, Thaw received permission to
hike twenty miles to a French airfield to see if he could
arrange to join the squadron based there. He failed in that
attempt, but made a favorable impression, and a month
later made the hike again. This time an officer in that
squadron told him that he would soon be transferred, and
on Christmas Eve of 1914 Thaw became a member of a
squadron known as *Escadrille D. 6.* He began as a backseat
machine gunner. As he met more French pilots, he asked
them to see if some of the Americans who had fought
beside him in the Legion could enter a French squadron
as he had.

Paralleling the efforts being made by Dr. Gros and Thaw
were those of twenty-eight-year-old Norman Prince, whose
father, Frederick H. Prince, was one of the richest men in
New England. Like Thaw, young Prince had learned to fly
in the United States before the war. During his childhood
Norman had spent summers on his family's estate at Pau, in
southern France, and he spoke French fluently. In January
of 1915 he set off for France, despite his father's opposi-
tion, and set himself up in a suite at the fashionable Hotel
Palais d'Orsay in Paris.

From that base, close to French government buildings,
this able and well-connected young man, a lawyer who
graduated from Harvard College in 1908, began to besiege
French officialdom in his quest to bring an America squadron into being. He found an influential ally named Jarousse

Fig 7. Norman Prince, known to his comrades as "Nimmie," was a rich Harvard graduate, another Founder and a man who helped to convince the French that an all-American squadron would be effective and help to mobilize American opinion in favor of entering the war. He died returning from a mission escorting Allied bombers whose destruction of the German Mauser rifle factory at Oberndorf showed the potential of air power.

de Sillac, a Frenchman his own age who held a prominent post in the Ministry of Foreign Affairs. De Sillac wrote this to a well-placed colonel in the French Ministry of War:

"It appears to me that there might be great advantages in creating an American squadron. The United States would be proud of the fact that certain of her young men, acting as did Lafayette, have come to fight for France and for civilization. The resulting sentiment of enthusiasm could have but one effect: to turn the Americans in the direction of the Allies."

These ad hoc American lobbyists—Dr. Gros, Bill Thaw, and Norman Prince, joined by twenty-nine-year-old Elliot Cowdin, a polo player from Long Island—initially encountered considerable resistance. They did not know that the French high command was, with reason, fearful that foreign pilots might be spies. Among other situations that had arisen, a German who spoke perfect French and had a forged

American passport had actually flown with a French squadron, been discovered to be a spy, and been executed. Another case had been that of F. C. Hild, an American who had joined the French Air Service early in the war. He soon deserted and returned to the United States, where he was suspected of selling French military information to the German Embassy. When Gros discovered these German connections and sympathies, it may have influenced his thinking about one of the requirements he set down for joining what became the Lafayette Escadrille: "You must be . . . not of German extraction on father's or mother's side."

At the same time that Thaw, Prince, and Cowdin went to work, Dr. Gros formed the Franco-American Committee, made up of prominent older men including Vanderbilt and J. P. Morgan, Jr.

Working separately, the two groups, one composed primarily of young enthusiasts and the other of seasoned businessmen, began to win over the French military authorities. In February of 1915 the Ministry of War agreed that Americans could enlist in the French Army's aviation service, and at the end of March, six Americans, including Thaw, Prince, and Cowdin, were assigned to begin pilot training. On July 8, 1915, General Auguste Edouard Hirschauer, chief of French Military Aeronautics, decided to have the French Army organize what would initially be called the *Escadrille Americaine*. Nonetheless, the bureaucracy continued to move slowly in making the transition from paperwork to an operational unit.

*   *   *

Surprisingly, the biggest breakthrough came that autumn, when Thaw, Prince, and Cowdin applied for the annual eight-day leave given to all members of the French Army. The standard arrangement was, for example, that a poilu might be given a paid two-day trip home from the Western Front to his home in Marseilles, eight days of paid leave at home, and a paid two-day trip back to his unit. When confronted by three Americans whose homes were in the United States, the French Army unhesitatingly bought them round trips by transatlantic steamer to and from the port of New York.

As a result, on December 23, 1915, when the SS *Rotterdam* docked in New York, among the passengers disembarking were Thaw, Prince, and Cowdin. All three wore chesterfield topcoats with velvet collars, and Thaw sported a black derby of the type worn by lawyers and businessmen who worked in nearby Wall Street offices. Tipped off about their arrival, a crowd of newsmen peppered them with questions. The three fliers minimized their roles—at that time none of them had shot down an enemy plane—but the press swiftly built them up to be heroic figures.

Most of the American public responded to these stories with interest and enthusiasm, but a combination of pacifists and German sympathizers seized the opportunity to point out that these men, now being lionized, were members of the French Army, fighting in a war in which American citizens were not supposed to be armed combatants. The editors of two pro-German newspapers sent Secretary of State Robert Lansing carefully worded protests, and one account had it that within days German secret service agents

Fig 8. Elliot Cowdin, Norman
Prince, and William Thaw in
civilian dress

began following the three men. But a quietly dramatic and
symbolic coincidence occurred even sooner.

The morning after he landed in Manhattan, Thaw came
into the barbershop of the exclusive Ritz-Carlton Hotel for
a shave. The man getting a haircut in the chair next to him
was Count Johann Heinrich von Bernstorff, the German
ambassador to the United States. They had met before the
war at parties whose guest lists included diplomats and
members of prominent American families. The fifty-three-
year-old von Bernstorff began gently scolding Thaw, who
was twenty-four years younger, telling him that he and his
two fellow fliers were breaking their own country's law
prohibiting them from fighting in a conflict in which the

United States was remaining neutral. Thaw kept politely silent as his barber continued shaving him. Then von Bernstorff took a sterner tone, adding that Thaw and his friends should voluntarily intern themselves, and spare both the United States and Germany an international incident.

By this time, with Thaw's shave completed, he rose, and the barber helped him on with his topcoat. Putting on his derby, he nodded to von Bernstorff. Using General William Tecumseh Sherman's famous phrase, he said, "Excellency, war is hell," and strolled out.

Von Bernstorff next made a formal demand that Thaw, Prince, and Cowdin be interned. Some accounts of what happened immediately thereafter implied that the three men were hastily shipped back to France on the next liner heading for Le Havre, but there is no question of the impact their days in the United States had in Paris. A pilot who had remained in France said of his comrades, "They had created a tremendous enthusiasm and a real sympathy for France in their brief appearance." In addition to the publicity favorable to the French cause that the interviews with the three Americans had created, the ferocity of the German attacks on Verdun that began soon after the men's return convinced both the French and the British of the need to bring the United States into the war as soon as possible, or the Allies might lose.

Six

The Odds Are Never Good: Clyde Balsley

On Sunday, June 18, 1916, two years after the First World War began, a mustachioed twenty-two-year-old Texas fighter pilot named Clyde Balsley walked toward his plane through the predawn mists of a big grassy airfield outside of Bar-le-Duc, France. Balsley climbed into the cockpit of his plane, a small single-wing one-seater French fighter called a Nieuport 17 C-1, with a top speed of 110 miles an hour. The United States would not enter the First World War for another ten months, but Clyde Balsley was the ninth pilot to join this new squadron composed exclusively of American volunteers. It would soon be renamed the Lafayette Escadrille, in honor of the Marquis de Lafayette, the young French nobleman who crossed the Atlantic to fight beside George Washington during the American Revolution.

For five months, long columns of French reinforcements and supplies had passed ceaselessly through Bar-le-Duc, on their way to support the French armies locked in combat with hundreds of thousands of Germans at the enormous Battle of Verdun. The one dirt road, the only route into the besieged city of Verdun, was just twenty feet wide, but the French Army was in the process of sending up this narrow artery a total of twenty-five thousand tons of supplies, carried by some six thousand vehicles. It was later estimated that two-thirds of the entire French Army passed up this road during the effort to save the city. For the French Army and the French public, that narrow road through Bar-le-Duc took on spiritual significance, and became known as "The Sacred Way."

The Battle of Verdun would become the most significant battle of the war. A total of 800,000 men, French and German, died there—more than the 650,000 Union and Confederate soldiers who died during the four years of the American Civil War. Verdun was an enormous test of wills—the Germans attacking and the French defending. The French military leadership was quoted as saying, "They shall not pass," and this rallying cry had a seemingly hypnotic effect on the badly bloodied soldiers. An American war correspondent who saw the survivors of a French regiment coming out of the battle for a desperately needed rest said that despite their glassy-eyed expressions and staggering steps, they were eager to return to the fight.

The ferocity of the fighting in the air above that epic struggle equaled that on the ground. When the battle began, the Germans had total command of the air above it: Their 168 planes, many of them manned by pilots who had close to two years of combat experience, constituted the greatest force of warplanes ever assembled. Among them was

Richthofen, "The Red Baron." To send a pilot like Clyde
Balsley up against this array on his first combat mission
was close to a death sentence, but as the battle for Verdun
progressed, more and more pilots, mostly French but with
increasing numbers of courageous American volunteers
such as the men of the Lafayette Escadrille, made the battle
in the air more nearly equal.

In retrospect, when the Germans failed to take Verdun,
that opened the possibility of ultimate French victory, but
immense obstacles remained. To relieve the pressure on
Verdun, a combination of French and British divisions had
been sent to open an offensive in the muddy valley of the
Somme River, well to the west of Verdun. This offensive,
begun on July 1, 1916, involved what remains the single
costliest day in the history of the British Army. That day
the British and their Dominion and colonial forces suffered
twenty thousand men killed and forty thousand wounded.
By the time the Allied command called off the failed offensive four months later, more than one million men had
been killed or wounded, and this enormous bloodletting
had pushed back the Germans only eight miles. The battle
for Verdun proved to be a battle of great significance, while
the slaughter at the Somme accomplished nothing.

Balsley wrote descriptions of himself. One of them began
with this:

"Five feet eleven—not a giant, but not a dwarf; and
I had always been proud of my shoulders. Muscles like
steel springs, veins bubbling with vigorous blood, teeth

sound and white, skin ruddy, eyes clear, hair on the jump but plenty of it—not bald, at any rate—and Mont Blanc [genitalia] sprouting lustily."

On this day in June of 1916, after months of training, Clyde Balsley was about to fly his first combat mission. In January of 1915 he had sailed from New Orleans to Europe aboard the freighter *Dunedin*, working as one of thirty "muleteers," caring for 630 mules. After Balsley reached France, he sent his mother a letter explaining why he had volunteered. He told her that he wanted to "see the war, and see it well . . . I can learn aviation, the newest game in the world, which will mean that I have learned a paying profession while on this trip . . . And, finally, I can take a man's part in this war for humanity."

Balsley's words were those of a high-hearted young man expecting a safe outcome to an interesting and profitable venture in a cause in which he believed. Even his use of the word "trip" suggested the idea of a cheerful excursion.

When Balsley first got to his squadron for advanced training, he made a poor impression. One of the American pilots, who already had considerable combat experience, later wrote this in a letter:

"You know we didn't think much of Balsley. It was because he is young and inexperienced, but when he got here to the Escadrille I began to like him better every day, as I saw he had plenty of good will to work and was not afraid . . . I understand that his mother is very poor, and was dependent on him to run their bakery business, when he left and came over here, and that now the family is in very hard lines."

Balsley took off at dawn in his plane, on the side of which his French mechanic had painted the "Lone Star" of Texas. He was accompanied by two other American pilots and the squadron commander, Captain Georges Thenault. The mission of these four fighter planes was to protect some slow and bulky two-seater French observation planes flying above the Battle of Verdun as it raged below them.

At eleven thousand feet, Balsley and the three other French fighter planes met a superior number of German fighters engaged in protecting their own observation planes. Balsley dove at a two-seater German observation plane, getting within two hundred feet before he fired his Lewis machine gun. The weapon fired once, and jammed. He wrote about those moments:

"A German was at my left, two were on my right, one was underneath me, and the [plane] I had first attacked was still behind me. From the silence of my gun they would know there was nothing to fear. My fight was over. I could only try to maneuver back to Bar-le-Duc, where my escadrille was stationed."

Balsley hurled his plane into evasive actions. "I began to loop; I swung in every direction; I went into a cloud. Bullets followed. One scratched my machine and I slipped away from the man who fired it, and threw the belly of my plane upward.

"I was then about twelve thousand feet up. It was while I was standing completely on my head, the belly of my machine skyward, that something struck me. It felt like a kick of a mule. With the sensation of losing a leg, I put my hand down to feel if it was still there . . . But as my [right] foot went back with the shock of the bullet, my left foot sprang forward . . . I fell into a spinning nose dive . . . My gun was still useless, my entire right side was paralyzed, and I was bleeding like a pig."

The "bullet" that hit Balsley was an explosive bullet like a small artillery shell and a particularly lethal form of ammunition that had been outlawed in various disarmament treaties. It had struck his right thigh, and pieces of the bullet and fragments of his own shattered bones had sliced into his intestines, kidneys, and lungs. Balsley fought against losing consciousness, and somehow managed a crash landing just inside the forward French trench line.

The moment he landed, being thrown several yards from his demolished plane, German artillery began firing close to him as he lay near the twisted wreckage. Balsley tried to crawl away, but found that the best he could do was to pull himself on his stomach by grabbing at handfuls of high grass. Four French poilus, foot soldiers of the type drawn from France's farm families, some of whom may have been manual laborers before the war, slid through some nearby barbed wire, and braving the shrapnel flying just above their heads, they brought him to safety. Balsley described those moments:

"Two took me by the shoulders, two by the feet. Then like a beast unleashed, my pain broke from its long stupor. Almost crawling to escape the enemy's eye, the four dragged me like a sack of grain. Through the long grass, over and under and across the barbed wire, my bleeding body sagged, and sometimes bumped the ground. The pain had now become such torture that I almost fainted. Oh, if only some enemy would see us, would shoot and end my hell!"

Carried out of an ambulance and into an overcrowded French evacuation hospital ten miles from Verdun, Balsley was rushed straight to the operating table because he was an American volunteer. As he lay in a hospital bed hours later, he saw the daylight around him fading swiftly, even though it was still afternoon. He knew that the wounded French officer in the bed next to him was named Jacques.

"Jacques," he gasped, "—quick! I'm dying. When I go to sleep, wake me!"

Each time Clyde Balsley's eyes closed, Jacques cried out, "*Réveillez-vous! Réveillez-vous!*"—"Wake up! Wake up!"

This continued for four hours. Then Balsley said, "It's all right, Jacques. I'm not going to die."

Slipping in and out of consciousness, he suffered from great thirst because the doctors would not allow him to drink water due to the wounds in his stomach.

"My cry for water was so intense that it absorbed every other sense. I wanted to hear water, see water, to feel it trickling through my fingers. So violent was this one longing that I was actually blinded. I did not at first see the man standing beside my bed. Then came to me one by one—the heavy, black hair, the great arms, and the sincerest eyes in the world. When I put them all together, I gave a groan of joy. It was Victor Chapman, flown over from Bar-le-Duc."

Seven

The Oddsmaker Is Impersonal: Victor Chapman

Chapman came from a rich family in New York City. Educated in both Europe and the United States, this great-great-great-grandson of John Jay, the first Chief Justice of the United States, had graduated from Harvard in 1913. A physically powerful outdoorsman with strong spiritual feelings and a deep aesthetic sense, Chapman was living aimlessly in England when Germany declared war on France in August of 1914.

By the end of September of 1914 Chapman was a foot soldier in the Legion, fighting in the trenches. In December he suffered his first wound, from a rifle bullet in the right arm. He continued his life in the trenches until August of 1915, when he learned that he was being transferred to the French Army's aviation service. He had not applied for this; it happened through the influence of his father, John Jay Chapman, and his stepmother's two rich brothers, then living in Paris, William Astor Chanler and Robert Chanler. The three men knew Victor better than he knew himself. He was soon flying as a backseat machine gunner and bombardier, enjoying it far more than ground combat, and in the autumn he began his training to become a pilot.

A comrade, one of the first seven men to join what became the Lafayette Escadrille when the French regulations changed and that all-American unit was organized in the spring of 1916 (they were known as "The Founders"), said this of Chapman: "Everyone considered him a remarkable pilot. He was absolutely fearless, and always willing and able to fly more than was ever required of him. His machine [plane] was a sieve of patched-up bullet holes." As a man, he had the reputation of being quiet, kind, and considerate. Balsley later spoke of him as a friend "whom everyone in our squad[ron] loved deeply," and another man called him "a lover of art and of life," adding that in combat with enemy pilots Chapman "attacked them, no matter how many there were or what the conditions." A pilot who roomed with him said, "There is no question but that he had more nerve than all of us put together."

The news that Balsley was alive and in a hospital had reached the Escadrille at Bar-le-Duc, and Chapman had flown over with Balsley's toothbrush. Then, as Balsley told it, they had this exchange.

"'Anything I can get you, old man?' said he, meeting my thirsty eyes.

"'You bet,' I said. 'They won't let me have any water.' The way I kept moistening my lips finished my appeal . . .

Fig 9. Victor Chapman, of New York City, another Escadrille Founder. As the unit slowly increased in size, all its pilots came to love and admire him for his generous spirit and valor. In this photograph his head is bandaged because of an enemy bullet that creased his scalp. Refusing to take time to recover, he set off on a patrol three days later and was mortally wounded—the first of the Escadrille to die in action.

"'How about oranges?' said he, and turned to my doctor, just at that moment come in."

The doctor said oranges would be fine, but that none were available within miles. Chapman responded that he would get Clyde Balsley some oranges, even if he had to fly to Paris to buy them.

Balsley recalled what happened after that.

"The next morning I woke from my hot, drugged sleep, to find my captain bending over me.

"'Well, *mon petit,*' said he, 'I have a present for you.' Could it be the oranges at last? I looked up expectantly.

Something in the expression of my officer's face drew my attention to the whole room. There was a deep hush, and through it I felt the eye of every man upon me. Then I saw for the first time that my captain was not alone. The major and colonel were with him.

"Suddenly the colonel stepped forward.

"'In the name of the Republic,' began he—he took from his pocket a large box—'I confer upon you le Médaille Militaire and la Croix de Guerre.'

"'For me?' I asked. 'What for?'

"The figure in its horizon blue gathered as if about to spring.

"'Pourquoi?' His light, racing syllables slowed solemnly. 'You are the first American aviator to be seriously wounded—for France. Suffering greatly as you must have suffered, you flew far over German ground to bring your machine back safe—to France. There is sometimes a braver thing than overcoming an enemy. It is overcoming yourself. You, my son, have done this—for a country not your own.'

"He bent down and kissed me on both cheeks. Then, as I wore no shirt, he laid the medals on the pillow beside me . . . In the solemn hush a cork popped. Madame, chief of the nurses, had produced some champagne, and was pouring a little in the glass of every man in the ward.

"'Vive le petit Americain!' she proposed, her eyes, as mellow and lively as the wine, smiling at me over the bottle.

"'Vive le petit Americain!' came back the cheers, some almost a bark of pain, some already feeble with death, as those specters raised themselves on their pillows.

"Now I knew what it all meant—those people grouped about me like the picture of some famous death bed. Yesterday I had seen two men decorated. Both had died within an hour. So my time had come!

"'*Merci*,' I responded at last in a scared voice. Then, to my own surprise, I heard my own voice adding firmly, 'But I'm not going to die.'"

The next day Chapman came back with a bag of oranges, and promised to bring more the following day. Chapman now had a big bandage around the top half of his head, for in the meantime he had flown a mission during which a German bullet cut through the very top of his soft leather pilot's helmet, leaving a deep gash four inches long across his scalp. The doctor at Chapman's base of Bar-le-Duc urged him to rest for some days before he flew again, but Chapman replied that with the battle for Verdun bleeding both the French and German armies, every man should give his all. As for Balsley, once he had consumed two or three oranges, he limped and lurched around the hospital ward as he handed out the rest of them to the other suffering patients.

One of the interesting facts about the war as it developed was that a good many parents of the more prosperous American volunteers, men and women who had been used to crossing the Atlantic for pleasure in prewar days, would come over to visit their sons who were now at war. As it happened, Chapman's father, John Jay Chapman, was in Paris on such a visit when Victor was wounded. Told of that, he said, "If Victor is killed in battle, I am resigned. I am proud that he joined the French Army, and I think that every American boy ought to do the same."

For the next several days, Victor Chapman kept coming back, each time with a bag of oranges and cheerful messages from his fellow pilots. On June 23, 1916, a week after Balsley was wounded, instead of Chapman returning with more oranges, another pilot brought him a bag of them. When Balsley asked after Chapman, the man told him that Chapman's plane had broken down.

A day later Clyde Balsley learned the truth. His friend, the wounded French captain Jacques, read him the story from a Paris newspaper. Chapman had been in his plane on the ground at Bar-le-Duc with two bags of oranges, ready to fly over to Balsley's hospital, when he saw three of the Escadrille's best pilots taxiing out to fly above Verdun.

The guns of the unit's planes were always loaded before any flight that took place near the front. Chapman decided to take off behind his comrades and join their mission before going on to visit Balsley. He soared into the clouds and could not find them. The three who had taken off ahead of him had no idea that he was trying to support their efforts. When Chapman finally caught sight of them, they were engaging several German fighter planes. He dove down through the battle, trying to distract the Germans and give his friends an advantage. Even then they did not see him. Outnumbered, they decided to break off and head home. With Chapman alone, three of the German fighter planes pounced on him, fatally shooting him down three and a half miles inside the German lines.

Thus, in a week's time, Clyde Balsley had become the first American aviator to be critically wounded in World War One, and Victor Chapman the first to be killed. When

Chapman's father, who had returned to New York, was told of his son's death, the elder Chapman said, "My son's life was given in a good cause." Chapman's body was not found until years after the war, but two weeks after his death the Fourth of July ceremonies at the American Church in Paris included a memorial service for him. Ranking French military officers and other dignitaries crowded the church, and the congregation included prominent members of the American expatriate community in Paris.

One of these famous Americans was J. P. Morgan, Jr. The younger Morgan, then fifty-one, had ample reason to hope that the Allies would win the war. In 1915, when it had become clear that the war would be long and bloody, he'd loaned the French government fifty million dollars. The Morgan interests also became the official purchasing agency for the British government, buying massive amounts of steel, chemicals, and other commodities and charging a 1 percent commission on all transactions. This was to be followed by Morgan's formation of a syndicate of more than two thousand banks that loaned the Allies five hundred million dollars.

At the request of the resident New York newspaper correspondents, the American volunteers in the Foreign Legion and those assigned to the French 170th Infantry Regiment, which had a reputation for valor almost equal to that of the Legion, had received a forty-eight-hour leave to attend the day's activities. This included a ceremony at Lafayette's tomb in the Picpus Cemetery in Paris.

Victor Chapman's death unleashed a torrent of Franco-American feeling. During a banquet in Paris that evening of

July 4, French prime minister Aristide Briand paid tribute to Chapman as "the living symbol of American idealism." Equally important in terms of enlisting public support in the United States for the idea of entering the war, the *New York Times,* in its issue of July 5, 1916, covered all the day's events. Two months later, on the occasion of the 159th anniversary of the birth of the Marquis de Lafayette, some eight hundred celebrities, including the Arctic explorer Admiral Robert E. Peary, gathered at New York's Waldorf-Astoria Hotel to honor France, in the person of its ambassador, Jean Jules Jusserand, who had this to say:

"Never in my country will the American volunteers of [this] great war be forgotten. Serving in the ambulances, serving in the Legion, serving in the air, serving liberty, observing the same impulses that brought Lafayette to these shores, many young Americans, leaving family and homes, have offered to France their lives. America has shown tonight that she does not forget; France will show that she remembers."

Critically wounded, Clyde Balsley had much more to endure. This was later described by his squadron mate Ned Parsons. When Parsons made his decision to cross the Atlantic to fight for France and asked his father for passage money, his father "flatly stated that it was not our war and he wanted no part of my wild scheme." Parsons then wangled a voyage from New York to the French port of St.-Nazaire as an "assistant veterinarian" aboard the *Carpathia,* a ship carrying two thousand horses, and spent most of his time shoveling manure.

Parsons went on to write two books. Their titles revealed his mixed feelings about his time with the Escadrille. The first was *The Great Adventure.* In his second, the sharp-edged *Flight into Hell,* he portrayed how Clyde Balsley's "trip" to "see the war, and see it well" turned out. Referring to the terrible wounds that Clyde received when he was shot down, wounds that kept him in hospitals in France for nineteen months, Parsons said:

"Although, after the removal of more than forty pieces of the [large explosive] bullet, plenty more still remain, and he is badly crippled for life, Clyde is a real hero and never utters a complaint. The glorious record of his great adventure is compensation enough for him, for he knows that, despite the pain and suffering as the first American aviator to be wounded, his services to France and the United States were incalculable. The sympathy that he created cemented a bond between the two countries that can never be measured."

The idea that the wounding of one man could accomplish so much might be questioned, but while the First World War had enormous battles that could be marked on maps, there were also battles for the allegiance of the mind. In this saga, the adventurous and colorful young American fighter pilots who fought for France before the United States entered the war seized the imagination of both nations. Those volunteers never saw themselves as propagandists, but made their powerful statement by sacrificing themselves in the silver skies of northern France.

Eight

Women at War: Alice Weeks

As early as the first months of the war, a number of Americans started individual efforts to help the Americans fighting for France. An affluent, well-traveled, silver-haired lady named Alice Weeks was living in Boston when the war broke out. In early 1915, accompanied by her maid, Louise, she crossed the Atlantic to be closer to her twenty-four-year-old son Kenneth, who had been living in Paris in 1914 and was among the first Americans to join the Foreign Legion. The circumstances of her crossing and the people she met even before she reached Paris demonstrated that she was an extraordinary woman traveling in unusual circumstances.

In a letter she started writing at sea and finished when she arrived in Paris, she said this:

"We are somewhere on the ocean, but the map which is always on steamers in normal times showing the progress, is not given as there may be spies on board . . . I have been watching them put fresh water and biscuit in the lifeboats, so we are getting ready for submarines." In the first letter she wrote from Paris, she finished her description of the trip. "When we landed [at Liverpool] there was a big Red Cross ship beside us that had just come in with the wounded [from France] and everywhere in the station they lay on stretchers waiting to be put on the hospital train which was beside ours. It was my first sight of war."

After a rough Channel crossing from England to the French port where the passengers were to take the train for Paris, Alice had a lengthy wait before she went through customs and an inspection of her passport and other documents.

"By the time I reached the train there wasn't a seat anywhere but at last a gentleman opened his compartment, invited me in and likewise a Frenchman and his wife. The train ran very slowly as we traveled through the war-scarred country. At times we were able to get out and walk about while the train stood for some unknown reason.

"Louise came to me during one of these intermissions and finding me alone, asked me if I knew who these new found friends were. I said no, and she informed me they were the Duke and Duchess of Teck, the [British] Queen's brother and his wife. I enjoyed my day with them for we were all day getting down to Paris. When we arrived in Paris they said to me, 'How lucky you are that you can go to a hotel,' for there at the station was a platform decorated with flags and people waiting to receive the Duke and Duchess . . . The last I saw of the Tecks was when I turned on leaving the station and they waved their hands at me."

Beginning her life in Paris, where for a time she could not see Kenneth because he was fighting at the front, Alice first did work among refugees of all nationalities. She described her dismay at what she experienced:

". . . the stories I hear are so pathetic, mothers who have lost children, and wives who are hunting for husbands, and wounded sons who do not know where their families are. It doesn't seem possible that this is possible in this day. I have known women to walk through the country a hundred miles to hunt for their families. I saw a soldier saved by his dog who took him out of his shell hole after being buried and many men with arms and legs missing. I wonder if this is not hell after all. Surely the people who inhabit the earth have only so far succeeded in veneering themselves. Underneath they are still the same old savages."

Alice and her son Kenneth had an affectionate bond. Along with a number of this first wave of American volunteers, he was a precocious intellectual. The London publishers Allen and Unwin had recently brought out his 190-page book of philosophy, "Science, Sentiments and Senses," all of which, except for the nine-page prologue, he had written by the time he was twenty-one. In it he foresaw this, at a time when concern for the environment was in its infancy:

"We know that water will finally disappear from the [Earth's] surface . . . the seas will dry . . . After this, our planet will go to join the ranks of Moon, Mars, and Mercury, cold and dead."

Kenneth also remained fully involved in the issues of his day. In a letter that he sent to his mother five weeks after he joined the Foreign Legion and was still in training,

Kenneth eloquently expressed the idealism motivating many men like him.

"It is commencing to grow cold, and no doubt this winter we will suffer, but through it all I will be satisfied if the victory is ours, and I would be glad to die in perhaps the most crucial test that civilization has ever experienced." As for how Kenneth saw the Germans, he wrote, "They have destroyed the Cathedral of Rheims—a pretty feat. Their ancestors destroyed Greece and Rome." At the same time he expressed a grudging admiration for German courage and discipline: "Big attack here three days ago; the Germans come on in columns of eight, and are mowed down in spite of it." Back in his idealistic vein, he closed another letter to his mother with this: "My dear, I embrace you with all my love, for in defending France I hope to defend you." Replying to one from her just before Christmas of 1914 in which she expressed fears for his safety, he said, "Much love, dear. I think always of you and the happy days that are to come. Be patient, and do not doubt of my happy return."

Despite his preponderant idealism, Kenneth shared some of his mother's skepticism about military ardor. In a letter to her written in May, he said, "Yesterday we had a review of the Division, and decorated several men. Parades of that sort seem abominably silly in hearing distance of the cannon; and what children we are to be pleased with medals and stripes!"

In a letter to her younger son, Allen, who was back in the United States, Alice described her refugee work in Paris.

"I am working at St. Sulpice, the old monastery which has not been used for ten years . . . It is a huge building with a courtyard and a tower with a clock which I think has stopped in astonishment to see so many women and children. Every [monk's] cell has a family in it . . . It is very sad to see so many lost children, and nothing can be done, for all letters are returned from [German-occupied] Belgium. My woman [a refugee she helped to support] saw her home burned and one child with it. Her husband is at the front and she is expecting a baby next month.

"I found among some soldiers there was one American boy who had been wounded and had no place to go. He was not well enough to go back to the army, or sick enough for the hospital. He spoke little French and when I found him I said, 'Well, my boy, what is the matter,' and patted his back . . . he began to cry. He is a splendid athletic-looking fellow, but his nerves are pretty high-strung and a little kindness was too much for him.

"As I was going out to dinner tonight, he came to see me. The British Charitable Society are sending him to England where he can find work. It is hard here as he speaks so little French. He had to go at once, and spent his last franc to take the taxi and see me before he left. I told him to write me, gave him some money, and felt sorry to see him go."

Alice had the satisfaction of a mother sending her son things to eat. In a note to an American woman friend, also living in Paris, she said, "Today I sent Kenneth sausages, figs, peanuts, jelly, crackers, prepared coffee and oranges and every week I send him chocolate."

As Alice's life in Paris unfolded, she became an adoptive mother to the group of American volunteers in the Foreign Legion, some of whom knew Kenneth. When they had short leaves they headed for her spacious apartment. She called them "my boys," and entertained them with good food and gave them the opportunity to take hot baths and have their mud-crusted uniforms laundered. Once her "boys" went back to the trenches, Alice sent them packages of food and such things as gloves, long underwear, and blankets.

Six of these men would become pilots in the Escadrille, and all of them regarded her as their *Maman Legionnaire*— Legionnaire Mother. At one point she wrote to her son Allen, "I have thirty men at the front now to look after, six prisoners [held in German prison camps] and six aviators." Her "boys" wrote her warm and appreciative letters, to which she unfailingly responded.

Some of these letters were of a kind that a Bostonian lady seldom received. One man who began writing her was Bill Thorin, a self-described "roughneck" from Canton, South Dakota, who before the war "had adventures as a marine on a Chinese gunboat and as a United States soldier on the Mexican border." In a thank-you note he told Alice that he and three of his comrades were in a military jail at the La Valbonne training camp because they had been in a brawl in a café. Far from asking her help, he seemed proud of the affair. "Some guys called us Americans a lot of fools and we smashed them up and then a gendarme on top of them. From what I hear from others, they have changed their opinion about us here in La Valbonne, anyway. It was a good go. Would not have missed it for anything. It is bad, though, we smashed up a lot of things in the café as well, so we have to pay twenty francs in damages, but it is four of us, so I guess we will get the money somehow." In a later letter he told her that the jailers were selling them an alcoholic concoction he and his friends called "Kill Me Quick," which he described as being "strong enough to start a motor car."

Alice's willingness to help those in need also brought to her those who were not Americans. To one of her woman friends in Paris she wrote, "This morning a [French] soldier came to see me. He had been eighteen months at the front, twice wounded, had never had a vacation except four days' convalescence. His family are in the invaded district and he has never heard from them. My letters and groceries were the first thing he had. He kept saying over and over, 'My, but it was good to get that letter.' He now is stationed in Paris making motors for aeroplanes. I gave him some socks and cigarettes and a little money and he went away happy, saying he had friends now in Paris."

She wrote to her son Allen of a similar experience. "A French soldier came to me the other day, and asked me to care for his two children who were with their grand-mother . . . their mother was dead. He didn't need any-thing he said, but I found out he did and fitted him out. His daughter he knows nothing about. She was lost in the beginning of the war."

In yet another friend-of-a-friend situation, Alice opened her door one morning to find a French soldier from Australia who had been given her name and address by one of her "boys." "He said that five of his brothers were at the front and that his mother had come on from Australia to be near them. He said, 'My, but it is nice having your mother back here when you are at the front.' I don't know the part that mothers played in other wars, but they play a big part in this."

Whenever Kenneth was sent from a rest area to the front, his letters became less frequent. In one he wrote at Easter of 1915, he referred to the lice and other vermin that infested the dugouts and trenches: "Also please send me a cake of camphor and a bottle of camphorated oil. I am going to try that for lice; did you ever have them?" After his mother sent him what he asked for, he told her, "Your bug water is no good; send the camphorated oil, not to kill, but to chase them." He declined her offer to send him a heavy sweater, saying "the less to carry the better. Do you realize that the sack [full field pack] alone weighs fifty or sixty pounds?"

Letters to and from the front moved slowly, amid reports of increasingly furious battles. On May 11, 1915, Kenneth wrote his mother a brief postcard:

"Dear Mother,

"Have been fighting hard for several days, and it's going on. Don't worry about me. We have taken enemy's trenches, but it's not over yet. Will send you a line as soon as possible.

"I think of you in the thick of it.

"Love, dear, and courage.

"KENNETH"

Alice later learned that Kenneth wrote that card on the battlefield during the taking of Neuville-St.-Vaast, a village near Arras in the northwestern corner of France. He handed it to a wounded soldier he saw crawling to the rear, and somehow it reached her in Paris. Increasingly worried about him, on May 18 she went to see "Monsieur Grandidier, private secretary to General Gallieni, who is Governor General of Paris." In the back-and-forth of letters between the front and Paris, a letter that Kenneth had written four days earlier gave her more recent and accurate information than she received through her connections at French Army Headquarters. Writing to Allen, she said of Kenneth's recent battle experience, "Only 1,800 out of 4,000 of his regiment came through." Also, with the thought that Kenneth's chances of survival might be greater in the air than in the trenches, she had been investigating the possibility of his being one of the first Americans to be accepted for pilot training. When she broached the subject, he reacted to it in a letter in which he first told her about the battle from which he had just emerged.

". . . we have been fighting hard, and fighting victoriously . . . We fought forty-eight hours and were then replaced, going to the rear as reserve—that is, what were left of us . . ."

Of himself, Kenneth said, "Not a scratch—that seems miraculous to me in such a hell of fire and shells . . . We fought well, and I am happy."

As for his mother's idea, "I don't think I care about the aeroplane service, dear. I will stay with my regiment." Two weeks later, he apparently changed his mind; in a postscript to a letter, he asked his mother, "Will you find out whether I can get into the Aviation Corps or not? Of course, I know nothing of aeroplanes, but I did once of motors, and I could study."

During this period, in addition to seeing if she could get Kenneth transferred to pilot training, Alice wrote her son Allen three letters. In the first she spoke of her continuing work with refugees. "The woman I am supporting with her family, the refugee, has a new baby, a boy, and he is to be named for the President of France and I am the Godmother."

In a letter dated June 6, she commented on the bravery of French women.

"I have never seen a tear in the street. Sometimes at a shop some girl has just received bad news and the girls pat her on the back and she proudly straightens and asks, 'What will Madame have?' This happened to me the other day. The soldiers are not all at the front."

In the last of the three letters, on June 18, she wrote Allen, "This is only a line to say I had a letter from Kenneth yesterday saying he was going to the trenches in the morning. . . . I have been keeping at him for two weeks to make out a demand for the airplane service. For some reason he has not sent it and says now that he will after this time at the front.

"I have a wonderful chance for him and heard directly from the Minister of War this morning, saying if Kenneth would send the demand it would be all right. You can imagine how I am feeling. I can only say I have done my best and pray he may come through."

*   *   *

The day before Alice Weeks wrote that hopeful letter, Kenneth participated in an attack waged by the remnants of his regiment at Souchez, another small town near Arras. After his unit broke through the first and second German lines, his comrades last saw him on June 17, 1915, "running toward the third line of the German trenches, his right arm extended, and facing the enemy." He had been trained to throw grenades, and running toward the enemy with "his right arm extended" was consistent with that.

An unimaginable time began for Alice. Despite her using every kind of connection and entering into a correspondence with his surviving Legion friends, no one had seen him since that bloody day, and she never received the usual Red Cross card sent to the families of those who arrived in prison camps on either side.

Partly to distract herself from her constant hope of news of Kenneth, she threw herself into her role as *Maman Legionnaire*. Her big apartment also became the wartime home of Paul Rockwell who had sent his brother Kiffin "The Bottle of Death." When the Escadrille came into existence, its pilots named Paul as their official historian. In that capacity, he made frequent visits to them at the different bases to which the squadron moved. The Americans in the Foreign Legion who wanted to become fliers rightly discerned that Paul Rockwell had considerable influence to expedite their applications for French aviation. In his rooms in Alice Weeks's apartment, he became a clearinghouse for everything from storing pilots' civilian clothes to arranging to have their photos of one another and their planes and girlfriends developed and sent back to them.

As the war continued, Paul Rockwell married a young woman named Marie Francoise Jeanne Leygues. Her father, Georges Leygues, was a deputy in the French parliament and president of that body's Foreign Affairs Committee, and he later became premier of France. She and Paul had a daughter. Thus the men who visited Mrs. Weeks had both the advantages of her friendly and comfortable surroundings and the opportunity to spend time with a combat veteran who was living a relatively normal family life.

Every young volunteer who came to Alice Weeks's house was grateful for her hospitality, but in addition to that she acted in a special letter-writing capacity. The Germans did not allow prisoners they had taken to correspond with their former comrades, so Alice became an intermediary, passing letters addressed to her on to the men named in them. A few of the men who visited her regularly developed particularly warm friendships with her. Kiffin Rockwell, Paul's brother, had been in Kenneth's squad of foot soldiers and was wounded in the thigh on May 9, nine weeks before the attack after which Kenneth went missing. Kiffin spent six weeks in a military hospital, and then convalesced for another eight days at Alice Weeks's apartment. She dressed his wounds and later wrote a friend, "He looks terribly with those dreadful eyes men always have after going through heavy firing. I can not describe them. They are sunken and yet have a sharp look."

Kiffin Rockwell was as great an idealist as one could find, and a man susceptible to martial ardor. When he was transferred into the Foreign Legion's First Marching Regiment, created specifically for men who enlisted in 1914, he said this of his new comrades, and of their behavior on the day of the attack in which he was wounded:

"They were more serious about the war, and the volunteers were men who engaged out of love and admiration for France, and because they knew they were *right*. They were men who had the courage of their convictions and were willing to die, if necessary, to prove it.

"So the day we were called upon to attack, every man went into it willingly with the determination to do his best, and humming the *Marseillaise*. As to the officers—no officers ever led their men better than ours led us. Practically every one of them fell, but they fell at the head of their men, urging them onward." In a situation that most men would find ghastly, he said, "All I could think of was what a wonderful advance it was and how everyone was going against the stream of lead as if he loved it."

Alice kept widening the circle of those she wrote in hopes of hearing about Kenneth. In a letter written September 3, a Legionnaire named Lawrence Scanlan, who was from Cedarhurst, Long Island, near New York City, told her this:

"Dear Mrs. Weeks,

"I received your letter yesterday and I am very sorry I cannot give you any information. The last I saw of Kenneth, he was running just behind Smith and Kelly, a little to one side. [John Smith's real name was John Earl Fisk, but the Legion allowed a man to change his name when he enlisted.] They were not very far from me, but when I was hit I fell down in a trench and so didn't see them anymore. That was at the third line of German trenches. That is what makes me certain that if Kelly was a prisoner, the others were also.

"I would have written long ago, but had lost the address Kenneth had given me. I understand how you feel and if I receive any news at all, I will write you. I thank you very much and will call on you if I need anything.

"Hoping I will soon have more news of Kenneth, I remain,

"Very sincerely,

"Lawrence Scanlan"

Near the end of August 1915, Alice wrote her son Allen a letter that conveyed the sensations of being in her apartment in Paris.

"It is becoming a meeting place and I get no chance for loneliness . . . My apartment is high and almost every day I can hear the boom of the cannons at the front. It is more feeling the vibration than hearing. They tell me it is the big cannon bombarding Compiègne [forty miles away]. I thought the other night that some heavy trucks were having difficulty in coming up the incline on the hill, but they turned out to be machine guns at the front. In the quiet these sounds go far:

"How much there will be to tell you when I see you again! Too much to write about. I would never get through.

As the men come in from different lines at the front, I begin to feel I know every division in the army.

"Mother"

Alice may not have known "every division in the army," but she heard some remarkable stories, one of them told to her by a man named Andrew Walbron who was serving in a French infantry regiment.

"He was wounded last Fall and was for some time in the hospital convalescing. At last he went back and found his regiment north of Arras. The men said, 'Well this is a good place, and there is nothing doing, and the Germans come over and give us cigarettes for bread.' . . . A few days later the front line trench was blown up by five German [land] mines, and all in the trenches killed . . . those Germans had come over and been friendly, all the time pacing off the distance between the lines to blow up the men they were friendly with."

On one rare evening when there was not a man in the house, Alice had this to say about her one pet:

"My kitten Coco is so lonely without the boys to-night she will not leave me and cries in a pathetic way. They are so rough with her I should think she would be glad they are not here."

On November 25, 1915, twenty-one weeks after Kenneth was last seen running forward in the attack at Souchez, his decomposed body was found there between the French and German lines. Alice did not receive the news for another five weeks. On January 2, 1916, she wrote this to her brother Fred in the United States:

"I have been notified this morning that
Kenneth fell on the Field of Honor June
17th . . . Don't worry about me. I am surrounded
by friends who try and smooth the rough places
for me. I shall, I think, have services here, and Paul
will write something for the Paris papers.

"I do not know what the future has in store,
but the boys cling to me and I could not leave them
just now.
"Lovingly,
"Alice"

To compound the tragedy, Alice continued to receive letters from her "boys," who for a time had no idea that her son had been killed. One from a friend who did learn of Kenneth's death came from Jim McConnell, who had been a brilliant and popular student at the University of Virginia, from which he'd been nearly expelled when he placed a chamber pot on the head of a statue of Thomas Jefferson just before it was unveiled in front of President William Howard Taft and other prominent figures. He was in pilot training, and the letter of condolence he wrote to Alice demonstrated the eloquence that readers would see in a book he subsequently published, *Flying for France*. McConnell told Alice, "After all these months of waiting that you have so bravely endured, such news seems too cruel to be possible . . . Taking everything into consideration, he made the greatest sacrifice that has been known in this sublime struggle that our France is going through. He was the best, his motives were the finest of any that volunteered for this fight for civilization and his martyrdom adds a greater content to the war."

Twelve days after receiving the news that Kenneth had been killed, Alice wrote her brother Fred about his memorial service.

"Friday I had a beautiful service here in St. George's Church (English). They offered it to me and were very kind. A friend of mine played the organ and the music was very uplifting. I said I would have nothing doleful and all the hymns were the kind that give you strength. I selected the lesson in St. Paul's Epistle, 'Though I speak with the tongues of men and of angels and have not charity—,' and the choir sang the anthem 'I will lift up mine eyes unto the hills.' And at the end the Hallelujah Chorus of Handel. . . .

"The French papers had a beautiful article about the service, saying I had given it for Kenneth and his comrades who fell with him, and ending with, 'To those young men who so nobly fell, the sympathy of all the mothers of France will be given.' Do you see why France makes us willing to give our lives for her?"

Great as Alice Weeks's ordeal was, a more concentrated form of agony awaited the mother of Lafayette Escadrille member Douglas MacMonagle, a high-living pilot from San Francisco. She was a resident of Paris who had thrown herself into war work as a volunteer nurse in one of the city's Red Cross hospitals. On a September day she was looking forward to having a brief visit with her only son at his air base at Senard, just to the east of Verdun. When she arrived at the nearby train station at Ravenel, one of his friends had to greet her with the news that he had been shot down and killed a few hours before. His plane had come down just inside the French lines. Several of Douglas's comrades had driven to the scene and pulled his body from inside the plane, finding him unmarked except for a small hole on either side of his head where a bullet had passed through just behind his eyes. They had brought his body back to the airfield and laid him out in an empty shed.

In a magnificent display of composure and courage, Mrs. MacMonagle entered the shed alone for a last visit with her son. The next day she stood bravely by his grave as trumpets played a final salute and a squad of riflemen fired three volleys as he was lowered into the earth.

An unfortunate situation occurred as she was about to board the train back to Paris. A man appeared, explained that he owned a local establishment frequented by the pilots—it was in fact a combination of bar and bordello—and presented her with her son's tab of ten thousand francs, or twenty-five hundred dollars. Mrs. MacMonagle arranged for payment, and went on her way.

Nine

More American Eagles
Take to the Sky

By the end of 1915, France had been at war for seventeen months, and American volunteers had been fighting at the front in the Foreign Legion for nearly as long. Nonetheless, with the doors of French aviation beginning to open before them, these veterans of brutal route marches and vicious trench warfare now had to take physical examinations for that branch of the service, as if French military officials had never seen them before.

Ned Parsons, who had been serving at the front in the American Ambulance Service before enlisting in the Foreign Legion, had to face these examinations. He had some defects, such as "being addicted to swollen tonsils, [and] the lid of my left eye drooped," as well as this: "Due to an unfortunate accident with a ring, I had lost the first two joints of the little finger of my right hand. That in itself, I gathered, would have been enough to bar me from American [military] aviation." He soon realized that the French

Fig 10. American pilot Edwin Parsons. One of the Escadrille pilots who survived the war, this picture shows him with a training plane at the Pau airfield. He is holding a hard leather crash helmet and flew combat missions wearing this mackinaw jacket, which was the type then popular on many American college campuses. Parsons also took to the air wearing *sabots*, the wooden shoes then used by European peasants.

military surgeons were carrying out a new policy: If these Americans want to fly, *voila*, let them fly.

A husky French military doctor, a major, told Parsons to strip down. Parsons quickly passed through a cursory examination of his heart and lungs, but feared the eyesight test. The major placed him ten feet from an eye chart that Parsons said had letters as large as a sign in Times Square.

"He commanded me to read. 'The second line,' he'd say, 'the third letter. I see there a *B*. What do you see?'

"Sure enough, it was a *B*, and I'd say so.

"'*Bon*,' he'd explode enthusiastically.

"Then we'd do some more of these silly exercises, he calling the letters as I checked up on him. He was right every time. He never tried to cross me by calling the wrong letter. He wasn't taking any chances I'd be wrong, and his '*Bons*' grew bigger and better with every answer.

"Then we passed to the color charts, where we repeated the same delightful process.

"'I see red. What do you see?'

"'Red, Major.'

"'*Bon*. I see green. What—'"

"But why go on? In two shakes of a lamb's tail it was all over. He gave me a friendly pat on the bare back that sent me staggering across the room and, signing his name to my papers with an official flourish, he congratulated me for being a perfect physical specimen and told me that as far as he was concerned I could go out and get myself killed at any time '*pour la France*.'"

At varying times, different Americans who had been serving as foot soldiers or driving ambulances were French military aviation, sent to one of four pilot training schools. Unlike what happened in the training programs of other nations, they often spent time alone in their planes right from the beginning of the three-month course, with instructors called *moniteurs* telling them how to taxi their "Penguins," the nickname for the planes that had their wings clipped so that they could not fly. Many flights in the air were solos, most in a Blériot, a plane designed by the young French inventor Louis Blériot, who made the world's first over-ocean flight when he flew from Calais to Dover in 1909.

The final exam in the first part of this pilot training consisted of two three-legged flights of 150 miles each. They had to be flown at a minimum altitude of three thousand feet, and completed within forty-eight hours. After that, the pilot had to pass his altitude test by maintaining flight for an hour at six thousand feet. (In flights of that height and higher, the pilots wore what some called a "teddy-bear suit." These were sometimes simply heavy fur coats, or leather fur-lined one-piece flight suits. The high-altitude outfit included fur boots, a heavy wool sweater, gloves, and what one pilot described as "a huge cork safety helmet which Wisdom tells him to wear and Common Sense pronounces impossible. Common Sense wins.")

Having passed all these tests, the pilot qualified for his *brevet militaire,* which involved a promotion to corporal and the doubling of his meager private's pay. Other courses such as navigation and aerial gunning lay ahead for him, but he received a four-day *permission* to go to Paris. There, many tailors were ready to help the new flier choose a uniform from among a variety of styles, any one of which cost the equivalent of fifty dollars. Once a tailor made it, a seamstress would sew onto the sides of the high collar of his tunic a pair of red tabs with a flier's embroidered insignia of a gold wing and a star, and stitch his corporal's chevrons on the sleeve. To distinguish him from men serving on the ground, a horizontal winged propeller emblem also adorned his sleeve.

Of all the Escadrille pilots, only Bill Thaw chose a true regulation uniform. "The rest of us," a pilot said, "went in for musical-comedy-style aviation uniforms, fearful to behold, and guaranteed to knock the not-too-difficult little mademoiselles right square on their backs. While the uniforms were entirely successful in their chosen purpose, they were hardly the thing for official inspections and always a bone of contention."

A number of students failed during this difficult training to become fighter pilots. Records of the Lafayette Flying Corps indicate that several were "radiated" out of that program "due to ineptitude," and reassigned to courses that resulted in their becoming pilots of bombers or observation planes.

In one case, an eager young American who had been fighting in the trenches and was accepted for pilot training ended his first solo flight by crashing into the top of a towering tree. For four hours he remained wedged inside the cockpit, physically unharmed but terrified that at any moment the branches precariously holding the plane might give way and drop him and his fragile aircraft to the ground. When he was finally rescued by municipal firemen from several miles away who brought long ladders and climbed up and got him down, "he asked for a transfer back to his original infantry regiment, where he could be safe."

Ten

There Was This Man Named Bert Hall

Some American pilots had been flying with French squadrons for months, but by the spring of 1916 the Escadrille was ready to enter combat as a unit. Thirty-eight Americans would fly in the Escadrille, every one of them entitled to be known as what the French called *"un numero"*—"a character." They presented an interesting demographic picture. At a time when to be "a college man" was a rarity, thirty of them either had college degrees or had attended college. That did not mean they all came from affluent families: a later study said that "fourteen were from families of average income; four rose out of the depths of poverty."

Sons of the American social elite were represented: Of the first seven pilots who reported in—those who became known as the Escadrille's "Founders"—two went to Groton and Harvard, one went to St. Paul's and Harvard, one went to the Hill School and Yale, one had been at the

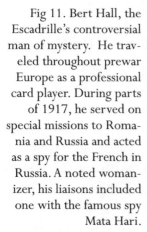

Fig 11. Bert Hall, the Escadrille's controversial man of mystery. He traveled throughout prewar Europe as a professional card player. During parts of 1917, he served on special missions to Romania and Russia and acted as a spy for the French in Russia. A noted womanizer, his liaisons included one with the famous spy Mata Hari.

University of Virginia, and another attended Washington and Lee. Those six were the sons of millionaires.

The seventh "Founder" was Weston Bert Hall, known as "Bert." He was a larger-than-life figure of mystery and legend. He was a slender man, five feet, eight inches tall, with a long thin nose, and photographs show his expression as varying between confidence and suspicion. At times he claimed to be born in Bowling Green, Kentucky, on November 7, 1880, making him thirty-five when the Escadrille began its official existence, but other records show him to have been born in Higginsville, Missouri, on November 7 of 1885.

Bert left home in his early teens and soon went to work as a section hand on the Rock Island Railroad. He went on to jobs in Kansas City and Dallas. By 1911, he had gained a wealth of experience from floating around the nation doing odd jobs. Most of his time had been spent in the Southwest, but he had been out to San Francisco, and up to Alaska. Later events showed him to be a skilled gambler, and he knew how to use his fists.

By the time he hooked up with the Escadrille, Hall had also been married and divorced twice. (His relationship with women was a story in itself. During his lifetime he is known to have had five wives, and may well have been a bigamist.) He had also competed successfully in automobile races held on the beaches of Galveston, Texas. In 1911 he was working as a chauffeur for a Galveston cotton broker named D. W. Kempncr.

In 1912, Kempner and his wife decided to go to Paris, taking their chauffeur Hall with them. Soon after they reached France, Hall quit working for the Kempners. As with many episodes in his life, one version has it that the Kempners fired him, and the other is that Bert saw Europe as a beckoning playground. He told colorful stories about his next two years. The efficiency with which he later cleaned out his fellow Escadrille pilots in card games supported his claim that he had used those two prewar years traveling throughout Europe, competing profitably in bridge tournaments and winning poker games. He became fluent in French, German, and Italian, and seduced many women.

Among those with whom he had (or said he had) liaisons was Mata Hari, the Dutch beauty and exotic dancer who was convicted of being a German spy and executed by a French firing squad. ("Mata Hari" was her Indonesian stage name. Her Dutch name was Margaretha Zelle. When Hall learned of her death, he wrote this in his diary: "I don't think I ever loved Maggie Zelle, nor do I believe she ever loved me, but it makes me feel all creepy when I think of her standing up before a firing squad, particularly after we had made such violent protestations of affection to each other, and had spent such wonderful times together.")

Bert Hall mixed with all levels of society, and could cut anyone down to size. When a socialite hostess took a condescending tone in asking him what his hobby was, he answered her with two words: "sexual intercourse." One account of his life, covering his activities in war and peace, described him as being "half hero and half heel." Another writer said of the difficulty in establishing the facts about Hall, "The problem for . . . the squadron's legacy was that Hall managed to outlive the six other founding members."

As the war began, Bert Hall was a taxi driver in Paris. Of the seven "Founders," five were dead by the time the United States entered the war in 1917. Bert Hall, however, went on and on, displaying his mental agility from the start. Enlisting immediately, he first fought in the Foreign Legion. When he took his French Army physical to become a flier, he knew that the man in line beside him, Bill Thaw, with whom he had been serving in ground combat with the Foreign Legion, had poor eyesight despite having logged many hours of successful flight before the war. He also knew that Thaw had been in France for more than two years and could read French very well. Hall gave this description of how things went when they appeared before the French eye doctor: "When he produced a French newspaper and held it up for us to read, Bill Thaw almost died . . . I went first so as to have time to think up something. When Bill's time came I told the doctor that Bill had not been in France very long and couldn't read a newspaper; therefore, a fair test couldn't be made with a French newspaper. 'Well,' said the doctor, 'are his eyes all right?' 'Surely,' I said, 'best eyes in the French Army!'"

Thaw was accepted for French military aviation. As for Bert Hall's mental capacities, in 1918, the last year of the war, a New York publisher brought out a book Hall had written titled "*En L'air!*"—every indication is that he wrote this book himself, based in good part on his diary entries. One study of his life calls it "his one true autobiography."

There is, however, another version of his experiences. In Paris, Hall met a Kentuckian named John Jacob Niles who was also a pilot. An accomplished musician, Niles was collecting some of the wartime songs. They reached an agreement that Hall would share his wartime diary with Niles, so that Niles could, as one account put it, "beef up" the diary entries and come up with something longer than the 152-page "*En l'Air!*" The result, published in 1929, was the 353-page *One Man's War,* billed as a collaboration between them and containing any number of episodes not found in Hall's first book. Intentionally or not, Bert Hall left a tangled factual legacy.

In Bert Hall's *One Man's War,* he described some of his training as an aviator, but it was left to another man, David Wooster King, a Harvard graduate from Providence, Rhode

Island, who had served in the Foreign Legion with Hall, to recount Hall's debut in French aviation. Hall had been telling stories of his prewar exploits as a flier. At the French Army's flying school at Buc, outside of Paris, "Bert climbed into the machine, had the controls explained to him, and started off . . . Full speed ahead, up, and then down with a crash. After they had extricated him from the debris the officer in charge questioned him.

"'What went wrong?'

"'I don't know.'

"'You don't know! Haven't you ever been in a plane before?'

"'No.'

"'What in God's holy name do you mean—starting off like that?'

"'Well, I thought I might be able to fly.'"

King concluded: "They decided he had enough nerve to be worth training." Nonetheless, knowing of his checkered past and thinking they might have another spy in their midst, during his early training the French authorities kept two agents pretending to be student pilots literally beside him, one sleeping on either side of his bunk.

Bert's learning curve as a pilot rose swiftly after his initial weeks in the cockpit. Before the next step, that of receiving advanced training to become a fighter pilot, he went to the Western Front as the pilot of an observation plane, which carried in the seat behind him an observer who tapped out radio messages in Morse code to French heavy artillery batteries on the ground. Hall described one of his earliest scouting missions.

"A volunteer was called for. I stepped forward, and with Lieutenant Manigal, who volunteered as my observer, hopped off.

"The weather was very cloudy and the ceiling was low. We crossed the lines so low that they shot at us with everything they had. Our wings were punctured in a dozen places. Under cover of the fog and the low clouds the Germans were bringing up some reinforcements. Headquarters had been advised of this through the Intelligence Department. Finally, after almost giving up our search we discovered that the report was well founded. At a point about thirteen kilometers east of Sommepy [140 miles northeast of Paris], the roads were jammed with all kinds of equipment, but mostly marching columns. This was our meat.

"We signaled our batteries, and the long-range gunners, who knew to a meter the location of every square foot of that country, opened up. The slaughter was something awful. Whole columns of Boche disappeared and wagon trains were splintered into mere heaps of tangled twisted junk. By flying back and forth, we gave the batteries closer ranges and they regulated their shots with amazing precision. The road I am telling you about runs perfectly straight after it gets out of Sommepy—perfectly straight for a long, long way. It was easy for the gunners, once they had the location right and left, to raise or lower the trajectory of their shots and sweep the road for miles each way.

"The ground rocked beneath us . . . We wanted to stay and see the end, but our gas was getting low, so we skimmed under the edge of the clouds, and dodging the fire from the ground, made our way back to camp.

"This story will give the civilian reader an idea of how important airplanes have quickly become in modern warfare. One airplane (and not a very good one at that), one pilot (more or less a green one) and an observer, with the cooperation of the artillery, breaking up the most carefully laid plan of the enemy; perhaps, saving the lives of hundreds of our own men and costing the enemy great losses in both manpower and equipment."

Before the war Bert Hall had been living in a small apartment in the Passy district of Paris, near the Bois de Boulogne. All was confusion as the war began.

"I never will forget the concierge who took care of the building. She came to me on Sunday morning (mobilization having been announced the afternoon before, and all the railways going east and north having been taken over by the Government) and said:

"'Monsieur Hall will be very patient with an old lady after this.'

"'Why, yes, Mother Pivot, surely I'll be patient with an old lady. Haven't I always been? Has something happened? Have I been *pas gentil* [unkind]?'

"'It is only the war.' Referring to her son, she added, 'Philip has joined his regiment. I must attend to the building alone now. Monsieur Hall will be very patient.'

"She seemed to be looking far off over the excitement and bustle of the terrified city—far off to a marching column of blue-clad figures. Her son Philip was in the column— Philip, who wanted to be an architect. He had been attending the Beaux Arts. The concierge had known war before. Her father was a veteran of [the Franco-Prussian War of] 1870. I tried to be impersonal about the situation, but I'm sure I was not. The old lady looked like a painting—she was wearing the usual little white starched collar that marked her Sunday costume from the things she wore on week days.

"'Yes, Mother Pivot, I'll be patient, and if I can do anything any time for you or Philip—'

"It was an old worn-out phrase, but to save my life I couldn't think of another thing. She bowed her little formal bow and went away. Later I looked into her little room where she sat beside the downstairs doorway. A small red candle was burning beside a picture of Christ. Not far away was a picture of Philip. It had been taken when he entered the Beaux Arts. As I went way downtown, I thought of what Mother Pivot had said, 'C'est la guerre.' It was the first time I had ever heard the phrase used."

Within two weeks, Bert Hall had enlisted in the Foreign Legion at a French Army office in Les Invalides, the former military hospital that housed Napoleon's tomb.

"Following the trip to the Invalides, there were several hours of frenzied packing. Mamma Pivot did everything she could to help, telling me about her Philip all the while. Philip had been in several engagements—rear guard actions, they called them, because by that time, the French Army was retreating.

"When at last my meager traveling kit was assembled and Mamma Pivot came to tell me au revoir, she kissed me very gently and told me to be a good boy and some other things I didn't understand. There was an exhilarating sense of youth about that old lady—her body had grown old, but her attitude towards life had remained young. Since the very first day of the war she had been rolling back the calendar until by the 25th of August, she was quite as active as any sixteen-year-old girl, even in such matters as kissing soldiers good-bye."

Eleven

New Commanders for a
New Form of Combat

The men of the Escadrille—American pilots and the French mechanics and other ground personnel—knew that there was a hierarchy that ordered their squadron to move from one part of the Western Front to another, but on the unit level their lives were in the hands of Captain Georges Thenault of the French Army.

Thenault was born in 1888, the son of a schoolteacher and his wife in the rural province of Poitou. A good student, he entered Saint-Cyr, the French Army's West Point, graduating in 1909. One of the few army officers who were interested in aviation, Thenault became a pilot in 1913, the year before the war. By mid-1915 he was the commander of the squadron designated "C. 42." One of his fighter pilots was Bill Thaw, who had finished his service in the Foreign Legion and was now a sergeant-pilot, and they became friends. By that time Thaw had become involved in the effort to create an American squadron, which was on its way to being approved. Thaw suggested to Thenault, who spoke good English, that he ought to apply to become the new unit's commander. With Thaw's help, Thenault got the job.

Thenault would never say that he regretted his decision to lead the Escadrille, but he could not have anticipated some of what he encountered. Evidently wishing these American volunteers to be handled gently, his superiors severely restricted his disciplinary powers. In his official statements, Thenault praised his pilots, but in a private conversation he said that they saw themselves this way:

"We are here, we are daredevils, and we don't need French discipline!"

A Canadian pilot who had done some drinking with the Escadrille gave a detailed description of what Thenault faced:

"From the point of view of discipline, the situation was practically impossible for the French. Imagine a body of financially well-off Americans—basking in the knowledge that they were volunteers from a neutral country, who habitually played no-limit poker, who imported unlimited booze and food and who composed a body of men far superior educationally and possessed a far greater knowledge of the world than their French companions in arms—a French commander would have experienced great difficulty controlling such a body of men [even] if they had been French citizens and fully subject to French Army regulations . . . [Thenault] seemed hapless to cope with such independent, high-spirited men."

In writing of their experiences, two of the Escadrille credited Thenault with tact and patience in dealing with them, but all of the men, including some French pilots who occasionally lived and fought beside the Americans, complained of the way he played the piano in their succession of little squadron clubrooms. One account pictured it this way: "Thenault would invariably take command of the ivories and churn out such a horrendous racket that even his faithful dog Fram would howl in protest to stop."

Despite criticism of Thenault, the captain had a gift for identifying the combination of reflexes, courage, and judgment needed in a fighter pilot. Rather than simply accepting the American volunteers arbitrarily assigned to him, he periodically went to the replacement station at Le Plessis-Belleville thirty miles north of Paris, where newly trained pilots awaited their orders, and interviewed them. He made a surprising choice when he picked Dudley Hill, of Peekskill, New York. Hill was blind in one eye, but memorized the physical exam eye chart, and was accepted for pilot training. His French instructors soon discovered his handicap, but they liked him, and came to believe he displayed such good reflexes and instincts—what one leading French pilot called the balance between "discipline and audacity"—that he could do as well with one eye as many other pilots could with two.

Thenault passed over several seemingly far better prospects to take Hill on. As one later account put it, Thenault had chosen, "in spite of his handicaps, a courageous, durable, unusually proficient flyer who logged more time (on the line ready to fly, or on patrol) than any other member of the Escadrille."

In addition to breaking in his novice pilots by leading them through the skies on their early patrols, Thenault took them for rides in a staff car through areas behind the front lines, pointing out flat open areas where they could land if they could not make it back to their home field. This would lead to some uses of these areas and those like them that Thenault did not anticipate.

One American pilot offered a picture of Thenault found nowhere else. Writing in his college reunion yearbook twenty-one years after he served in the Escadrille, he said this of conditions the squadron faced while serving at an airfield right on "the North Sea Front with the British. Life in mouldy, wet tents on the beach. Our Captain sets up his headquarters in a bawdy house, the only warm place always open."

As commander, Thenault had some encounters he could not have imagined. A German single-seater fighter plane had an engine failure and landed at a base the Escadrille was using. The pilot got out of his plane, came into the squadron headquarters, and asked to speak to the commanding offi-cer as soon as possible. When Thenault appeared, the enemy pilot saluted and formally surrendered. In good French, he told Thenault that his plane had an explosive device attached beneath its fuselage that would blow up the plane fifteen seconds after a timer was turned on. That would give the pilot time to run some distance away, but prevent a captor from making further use of the plane. He had not started the timer, and wanted the squadron's ordnance men to know that they were dealing with something dangerous.

Thenault thanked him, and asked why he had not acti-vated the timer. His prisoner replied, "Mon Capitaine, it is a new invention and I'm no fool. I've seen these new inventions go off at the wrong time before now. I'd like to destroy my ship, but I have no faith in new inventions."

Twelve

Shadows of War in the "City of Light"

For Parisians, the war unfolded in phases. First came the crisis in September of 1914, during which Paris taxis and buses rushed reinforcements to the dramatic defense at the Marne, which saved the city. Then a surreal calm descended upon its beautiful tree-lined boulevards and great stone monuments. By the spring of 1915, black armbands on the sleeves of older men marked those who had lost a son or grandson killed in bloody trenches fifty miles away, and the streets were filled with bereaved women wearing black. One account of that time said, "For a woman to dress brightly in the latest fashion was to invite the scornful glances of passersby who well knew the price in blood that France had paid each day to keep the city free."

The Germans occasionally attempted a night air raid on Paris. During one of these, a zeppelin attack, pilot Alfred Holt Stanley, from Elmira, New York, dashed into a darkened doorway to avoid falling bombs. He ran headlong into the arms of Laura Melvin, an American girl working for the Young Women's Christian Association as an interpreter and ambulance driver. A few months later they married, in Paris.

Only with the beginning of the horrendous Battle of Verdun in the spring of 1916 did the sights of war become common on the capital's streets. In a letter back to the United States, Alice Weeks wrote this:

"There will be no end of artificial legs needed. You see sometimes five or six men walking together, all with one leg apiece . . . Somehow you don't see as many armless. This is not so bad, it is only when one sees part of a face gone, that is terrible.

"As I write a regiment is passing going to the front with the band playing the *Marseillaise*. Poor fellows, but I am glad to see they are not boys. There are also horses with rapid firing [machine] guns strapped to their backs, ending up with a string of ambulances."

In a later letter, she said:

"Paris is beautiful now, for summer has come at last and today is almost too warm. I walked to the Bois and sat there for an hour . . . I met a young man and woman, dressed in light clothing and thought as they came toward me how well they looked, until I saw he was blind. She looked so happy to have him, even without his eyes, but what a long future before them."

In addition to benefiting from the decorous hospitality offered by Alice Weeks, many Americans had spectacular weekend leaves in Paris. Once the French patrons of a bar, restaurant, or bordello realized that a group of young men in French uniform, no matter how low their rank, were Americans fighting for France, every subsequent drink or meal or other entertainment was on the house. When such a group appeared at the theater, the entire audience would rise to cheer them. One of the Americans noted in his diary that he had been taken to the Folies Bergère to see its famous chorus line perform a dance that was the talk of Paris, called "*La Ceinture Chaussée*"—"The Dance of the Chastity Belts." Others simply noted in their diaries that they had horrible hangovers after drinking in the upstairs bar at the Chatham Hotel, or at the New York Bar, the latter destined to become the first of the many bars around the world called Harry's Bar.

A number of young pilots lost their virginity at what became known as "the Lafayette whorehouse" at 22 Rue de Berri, near the Arc de Triomphe. Henry Jones of the Escadrille, a pilot known for his resourceful substitute for hard liquor when it was not available—"bay rum, olive oil, and vinegar"—said of a fledgling pilot he took to 22 Rue de Berri for his first sexual experience, "I encouraged him, and he took to it very well."

Sadly, some of the initiates did not take to it well. A few contracted venereal diseases, which caused them to be dropped from the French Air Service, and one young man who could not face his condition committed suicide.

Thirteen

Things Are Different Up There, and Then on the Ground

As the Escadrille's pilots logged additional hours of aerial combat, its pilots began to experience more of the strange sorts of things that happened fighting in the skies. After all his training, one pilot got into a dogfight in which planes of both sides were whipping past him in every direction, firing the bursts of machine gun fire that marked these lightning encounters. He finally got behind a German fighter plane, opened fire with his Lewis gun—which was capable of firing ninety-seven bullets a minute—and had it jam on him after it had fired only four. To his astonishment and relief, those four bullets killed the German pilot and brought down his plane.

Another pilot saw a French plane catch on fire, with the German pilot who had rendered it helpless watching it about to fall to earth. The French pilot deliberately turned and crashed into his opponent, sending them both to their deaths.

The Escadrille's pilots became used to the bursts of black smoke caused by enemy antiaircraft fire, but Ned Parsons was startled when, as he described it, "Suddenly, out of the corner of my eye, first on one side, then the other, I caught a glimpse, not twenty feet from either wing-tip, of two elongated, bottle-shaped objects hurtling through the air and going in the same direction, passing me so all that I had was just a flash and they disappeared."

What he saw was a pair of artillery shells that had been fired from cannons on the ground, on their way to distant targets on the ground. "[They] must have been nearly at the top of their trajectory and at the point of inertia or I wouldn't have seen them at all." He was shocked "when I realized what these objects were and what would have happened to me had I been a few feet on one side or the other."

During a combat mission a pilot named Andrew Courtney Campbell, a bagpipe-playing young man from Illinois whom another Escadrille pilot described as a prankster "to whom trouble seemed to gravitate as naturally as iron filings to a magnet," managed to get the fixed-in-place wheels of his plane jammed through the canvas fabric of the upper wing of the biplane being flown by one of his squadron mates. There they were, stuck together and flying in the same direction. In a desperate attempt to extricate both of them from the crisis he had created, Campbell managed to use full power to soar away, tearing his plane's wheels out of the canvas wing below him. The pilot in the lower plane managed to make a crash landing from which he walked off unharmed. Campbell landed shortly afterward, treating the whole thing as a joke. Twelve days later, he was shot down and killed.

In the heat of combat, some men became capable of astonishing acts. A German antiaircraft shell passed through a French two-seater piloted by an American. The antiaircraft shell exploded, beyond the plane "but did not put the plane out of order, although it took the pilots' foot entirely off. He reached down and took up the foot and threw it back to the observer behind him, saying, 'Throw that at the damned Boches,' and brought the airplane down safely. He is now back again with a wooden foot, flying."

Occasionally situations occurred that left men on both sides bemused. During the spectacular loops and turns that occurred in a dogfight above an airfield the Escadrille was using, a German pilot lost a fine fur-lined flying glove, and it came floating down near a hangar. One of the American pilots picked it up—at that time in the Escadrille such a glove was "an unheard-of luxury"—and thought how nice it would be to have another glove as good as that. The next day the German pilot came zooming out of the sky at the risk of his life and dropped the other glove. Inside it was a To Whom It May Concern letter written in good English that said having only one glove was doing the German pilot no good, and expressed the hope that whoever now had both of them would fly safely and have good luck. The American pilot "was delighted to accept his gift, dropping a note of sincere thanks to the donor."

*   *   *

As more time passed, the hours in the air proved to be increasingly far from glamorous. Ned Parsons wrote this vivid description:

"Take a ship up to fifteen thousand feet, sit there for two hours immovable, and mere words are difficult to describe the pure agony of mind and body. The sub-zero temperature penetrated the very marrow of your bones. Despite three or four pairs of gloves, fingers coiled around the stick [control column] would be paralyzed in five minutes. Then they would have to be forced open and pushed away from the stick with the other hand and the paralyzed hand beaten against the side of the fuselage to restore circulation. A few minutes later the process would have to be reversed."

It was not much better on the ground. The cold of some bases was so intense that when a plane landed, the engine had to be kept running the whole time it was there or it wouldn't restart.

There was the problem of breathing. At fifteen thousand feet an additional supply of oxygen was imperative. In Bert Hall's book "*En l'Air!*" he described how pilots coped with this:

"We also carry oxygen tubes . . . Your heart will stop working without oxygen. We have rubber tubes and when we get to feeling a little giddy, we stick this tube in our mouth and blow ourselves up. One charge of oxygen will last about fifteen minutes."

Parsons described other elements of discomfort, bordering on torture:

"Feet were twin lumps of ice, rigid and unfeeling; shooting pains throughout the entire body, eyeballs and teeth smarting and burning, icy scalp contracting till it felt as if the skull must burst through and explode in a shower of bones, heart pumping half-congealed ice water instead of warm blood—thus it can easily be understood why liquor was a necessity. Without it, a man might easily come to earth a frozen corpse."

There it was. Liquor. Parsons emphasized, "When I say necessity, I mean necessity without qualification." He carried a half-pint aluminum flask filled with brandy in the breast pocket of his flying suit. "With judicial nipping, [the brandy] would just about hold out for a two-hour patrol."

After the Escadrille had been fully operational for two months, certain physiological and psychological problems common to all fighter pilots became evident. Simply flying at freezing high altitudes in cramped, open, unheated cockpits without plentiful oxygen placed their bodies under the great stress that Ned Parsons described. A German pilot wrote that sleep is "the food of the nerves," and many pilots found themselves sleeping ten and twelve hours a day.

When it came to relieving psychological stress, Parsons viewed alcohol as a friend on the ground as well as in the air. He said that he had never seen a pilot so hungover that he could not perform his duties, but he believed in alcohol as a sedative. "Few people," he wrote, "realized how necessary alcoholic relaxation was for nerve-strained aviators." After the first flight in which he heard strings of German bullets snap past his head, "I set my wheels down on the home tarmac and attempted to hop nonchalantly out of my ship. My knees absolutely refused to support me. They gave way like two pieces of string, and I had to wrap a shaking arm around a strut and hang on for dear life for over a minute. My sympathetic head mechanic, Felix Henriot, thought I had been shot through the body at least a dozen times. My face was greenish yellow, and my wildly staring eyes strained through two smudged circles that resembled holes in a blanket."

In the months that followed, when many Escadrille pilots had to spend two or three two-hour patrols in the air every day, Parsons found that "I wasn't sleeping nights. Flocks of planes chased themselves around in my tired brain all the time. I should have been thoroughly relaxed. Motors roared and machine-guns snarled. I pictured on a vivid background the combats I had fought during the previous day, the mistakes I had made, and visualized what I should try to do in the next fight to get more Huns. Frequently I got up for [dawn] patrols with the wambling twitters, and I was quite likely to burst into tears if anyone spoke harshly to me, or do a backflip if anyone dropped a shoe. A couple of shots of light stimulus and the wibble-wabbles quieted, and they didn't make a Hun too tough for me."

These haunting moments followed many pilots after the war. Captain Elliott White Springs of the Lafayette Flying Corps, a man who shot down eleven enemy planes and later became the postwar president of the Springs Mills textile giant, said this of himself: "Sober, I'm a nervous, serious-minded, conscientious, cold-blooded wreck, who lives in the past with my mind amid the triumphs and thrills and noises of the front, still feeling the fears and anxieties . . . But give me liquor, Ah . . . and I become a cheerful, optimistic little fellow . . . I get almost human."

All these strains inevitably affected morale. When these able, intelligent young men encountered realities like fly-ing without parachutes and seeing men being burned to death as a fighter plane spun its way thousands of feet to the ground, it produced such reflections as this, written by Ned Parsons:

"None of us had any real idea of what we were getting into. We had hold of the bear's tail and no one to help us let go. With few exceptions, I believe most of us would have welcomed the opportunity to bow out gracefully . . . We were merely very wild but very frightened youngsters, fighting with unfamiliar weapons in a new element, leaping to fame, and being made heroes overnight by newspaper publicity . . . Our sole claim to heroism was in being half-scared to death and doing our best in spite of it!"

Surrounded by every kind of fatal violence, Charles Dolan, the son of a Boston politician and the one man in the Escadrille who did not drink, said, "There was no one in the Escadrille who expected to survive the air war. It was not a question of would you die, it was just when!"

Ned Parsons saw it a bit differently. Speaking of the German fliers, he said, "Our adversaries in the air never represented personalities to us . . . our aerial battles were just like a game, with the personal element entirely lacking. But it was a game played for high stakes, and the penalty was death."

Fourteen

Bert Hall Takes Life by the Horns

After finishing his advanced training to become a fully qualified fighter pilot, on Bert Hall's first combat mission in the
northeast of France he saw a two-seater German observation plane called an Albatros, a craft differently configured
from the single-seat Albatros fighter. He attacked the enemy
plane, hitting it with machine gun fire, and maneuvered it
into a position very close to the ground. With the observer
wounded and sprawled unconscious in the backseat, the
enemy pilot was ready to surrender. Hall explained what
happened then.

"When we passed over the village of Suippes, I indicated a field south of the railway near the main road. The
German apparently understood and proceeded to make
a very fair landing. Through watching the enemy plane, I
didn't take very good notice of the ground and was forced
to make another tour of the field before making my landing.

"When I finally jumped out and ran over to the German plane, I saw the pilot was about to apply a lighted match to the underside of the fuselage, the portion just below the engine. The fabric at this point is always oil-soaked and will burn very easily. About twenty meters away lay the observer; he seemed to be breathing his last.

"It was a time for quick action. The thought of that beautiful German Albatros going up in smoke was particularly distressing. Our squadron hadn't brought home so perfect a prize, and now it was about to be burned by a fellow who I might have bounced off in the air.

"The German saw me coming. He did his best to hurry up the fire, but I swung a terrific right and landed my fist on the point of his chin. There was no bonfire that day. Some French ambulance men took care of the wounded observer and when the pilot regained consciousness, a detachment of French soldiers made him their prisoner. And was that pilot sore! He raved like a wild man! The idea of a German officer being struck in the face! The idea of carrying on warfare with one's fists! It was inconceivable!

"I was merely amused . . . I did explain to him, however, that I had used my fist instead of my automatic [pistol]. I might have finished him off in the air, or from a safe distance on the ground. But the German idea of a sporting chance didn't seem to involve a fistfight.

"When I landed the [captured] Albatros on our field at La Cheppe, there was what the French call a crisis of excitement . . . Best of all, Marshal [Joseph] Joffre had witnessed the entire procedure and was pleased no little bit—it was the first [aerial] combat he had seen up close—not that it

was much of a combat, but that it turned out so successfully for the French."

On his way to a record that included shooting down four
German planes and assisting his Escadrille comrades in
several of their victories, Bert Hall became involved in a
bizarre situation that might have become the worst international incident of the war. He and three other pilots "were
given orders to convoy a group of bombing planes over to a
German railway center where some troop movements were
reported." The bombers were from Britain's Royal Naval
Air Force, which had been created by Winston Churchill,
First Lord of the Admiralty. They were stationed on the
other side of the large grass airfield at Luxeuil, to which
the Escadrille had been returned for further duty.

When Hall led the four Escadrille planes to the point
where they were to meet and escort the British bombers,
he realized that the Royal Navy flight leader had made a
terrible mistake. His instructions had been to head for the
smoke from the factories and railway facilities at the German city of Mulhouse, but "they were lost, and were about
to bomb Basle [Basel], Switzerland, instead of Mulhouse,
Germany . . . If those Britishers couldn't be stopped before
they dropped their bombs . . . [the] Lafayette Escadrille
would be in disgrace and the Royal Naval Air Force would
be court-martialed from hell to breakfast . . . As soon as I
caught up with the British bombers, the leader of the flight
waved to me and was very pleased, but he kept right on
going. Basle, Switzerland, in ten minutes! I fired my guns

and did acrobatics to gain their attention. They wiggled their wings and waved at me . . . I wanted to strangle every one of them.

"At one time I really considered the possibility of diving at the leader and colliding with him, or shooting him down before I should allow the unnecessary slaughter of innocent Swiss civilians. But finally something snapped . . . The flight leader fired a Very pistol signal [a flare]. The bombers turned around as one man and flew back to Luxeuil as fast as they could.

". . . When we got back to the field, I landed first and waited for the Limeys, to see what sort of story they would put up. Finally they came, Sopwiths, Farmans, and all. Still I waited. Do you-all know those Limeys weren't even going to mention what happened? When I broached the subject, one of them said: 'Oh, yes, old man, thanks awfully for putting us wise. It would have been goddamned awful to crash in those poor Switzers. They would have been writing diplomatic notes two years from now.'"

Fifteen

Aces

The greatest of the Americans to fly for the Escadrille arrived quietly. A fellow pilot described Raoul Lufbery: "Broad forehead, deep-set eyes, squat, chunky figure just a trifle over five feet six and muscles of steel. He rarely ever talked, but when he did, it was with a strange accent that had traces of every nationality with which he had been in contact." Born in France in 1885, at the age of twenty-three in 1908 Lufbery had begun years of prewar travel that took him successively to Wallingford, Connecticut; Cuba; New Orleans; San Francisco; and innumerable other places. Still a French citizen, he eventually enlisted in the United States Army and served in the Philippines, thus becoming a naturalized American citizen. In an indication of what was to come, during his Army service he was the best rifle shot in his regiment of a thousand men, at a time when the Regular Army prided itself on its marksmanship.

After further travels to Japan and China, when Lufbery was in India in 1912 he met Marc Pourpe, the famous French flier whose acrobatic maneuvers thrilled crowds at early air shows. Lufbery became Pourpe's mechanic and close friend; together they toured Egypt, where Pourpe made a famous pioneering 1,250-mile trip from Cairo to Khartoum.

Bert Hall, who became a good friend of Lufbery's when they served together in the Escadrille, said that Pourpe had described Lufbery in these terms:

"He was a walking encyclopedia. He could tell you about any city that amounted to a damn anywhere in the civilized or uncivilized world. He could tell you how to spell the name of the city, where it was located, when the train left, what the jails were like, how the police treated gang fighters, if the food was any good; in fact, he could supply any information needed by a soldier of fortune, and that's what Luf was."

Pourpe and Lufbery were in Paris in the summer of 1914 so that Pourpe could pick up a new plane to perform in additional air shows in the Far East, but, with the start of the war in August, Pourpe became a French military pilot, and Lufbery served as his mechanic. In December Pourpe was killed coming in for a night landing in a fog. The Germans had nothing to do with the accident, but Lufbery swore vengeance upon them. He found his way to the Lafayette Escadrille, where his friends called him "Luf." Another Escadrille pilot said of the inscrutable future ace:

Fig 12. Raoul Lufbery was the squadron's leading ace, with seventeen enemy planes shot down. Born in France, this adventurer gained naturalized American citizenship by serving in the United States Army in the Philippines. His future fame in the air was foreshadowed by his being the best marksman in his infantry regiment of a thousand men.

"I only know one certain thing about him: Raoul Lufbery flew, fought, and died for revenge."

Luf also had a passion for mushrooms. Bert Hall said, "Lufbery is a mushroom hound. Every time it rains he goes out and gathers some mushrooms. The French say he is going on a *reconnaissance des champignons*."

During his time working and traveling with Pourpe, Luf had become a skilled mechanic, and brought all his practical knowledge to the Escadrille. Ned Parsons remembered this: "He spent hours at the butts [firing range], firing and regulating his [machine] guns, so that there would be no jams. He had his cartridges triple calibrated, thus eliminating to the greatest possible extent the chances of an oversized shell sticking in the breech-block."

The less experienced pilots found themselves in desperate situations from which they were saved by those more gifted than they. A pilot praised Lufbery's ability to rescue his comrades:

"He had a happy faculty of being on the spot at the right moment to rescue some unhappy buzzard who had gotten himself into a jam . . . Oft-times sacrificing a sure kill of his own, with his uncanny faculty for watching everything that happened in a dogfight, he'd sweep through the lead-filled sky to some isolated spot where a desperate youngster was waging a losing fight. Making a lightning decision as to his best method of attack, he would dart here, there, and everywhere, till it seemed as if the whole sector were full of Lufbery-piloted planes. Twisting and turning in a succession of amazing acrobatics, firing a short burst at one, then another, he bewildered and confounded the enemy hornets. No odds were too great in an emergency."

At times it seemed as if the odds *were* too great. When Lufbery came back from a draw in a dogfight with Oswald Boelcke, a leading German ace whom Richthofen considered to have been his mentor, his plane was "so thoroughly shot up that it was junked as being beyond repairs." As for Lufbery himself, it was found that "two bullets went through Luf's flying suit and one through his fur-lined boot."

On another occasion he landed at Luxeuil with "four neat bullet holes in his instrument panel, two on each side of his body, so perfectly in alignment that a deflection of a

Fig 13. Captain Oswald Boelcke, von Richthofen's instructor and mentor. Himself the victor in forty "kills," he died two years before von Richthofen when he and his wingman crashed into each other while chasing a British plane. Ironically, Boelcke had developed the doctrine that two planes should never converge on a single enemy.

fraction of an inch either way would have put them squarely into his brave heart. Luf always said that he was glad he didn't take a deep breath at the wrong time. In addition, there were twenty-two more neat holes stitched in his wings and fuselage."

As for how he had become what he was, a squadron mate offered this: "His air work was incomparable. It didn't come easily, for he wasn't a natural-born flier. He gradually and literally 'pulled himself [up] by his bootstraps' till he became the master craftsman. Then his plane became a part of himself, a thing that can be said of but few airmen. He flew as the bird flies, without any thought of how it was done."

Captain Thenault felt that Lufbery was made of some special material. He wrote, "To fly high is very fatiguing, as the sudden changes of altitude tire the heart. But never have I met a pilot with more endurance than Lufbery. When the sky was clear he would go up to eighteen thousand feet just for his own pleasure . . . Never was he at all ill from it. He was a superman." Utilizing Luf's combination of fortitude, skill, and intuition, Thenault repeatedly sent him to higher altitudes, above where the other pilots were patrolling, to "dominate the situation."

Thenault saw Lufbery as a man always poised and calm, but on one occasion he received a telegram from Lufbery saying in sketchy French, *SUIS RETENU DANS UN DISCIPLINAIRE PLACE DE CHARTRES*—"I am held in a jail in Chartres." Lufbery had been standing on the first-class platform of the station in that cathedral city when a ticket collector, doing his job, asked him for his identity papers and his ticket. In doing so he brushed against the seemingly unflappable Lufbery, whose nerves snapped. He attacked the man, punching him to the ground as he knocked out six of his teeth. Thenault wired the military authorities at Chartres, asking them to release a man who had done worse than that to a number of German pilots.

Other than an evident dislike of being touched unexpectedly, one great fear haunted Lufbery. Bert Hall described a postflight talk he had with Lufbery, in which Hall told him about attacking a German photographic plane above Verdun. The enemy observer had put some bursts of machine gun bullets through the top wing of Hall's biplane, but, as Bert wrote of what happened to the enemy pilot, "When flames burst from his forward cockpit, I knew it was all over."

Lufbery asked, "Afire, Bertie?"

"Yes, Luf, right over Fort Douaumont."

Lufbery's response to that was, "God, it's awful to burn up in the air. I'll never do it. I'll jump first."

Luf became involved in a unique situation. At different times, pilots of the Escadrille would be sent to Paris to pick up new planes. On one occasion the men who had just arrived in the city included Bert Hall and Lufbery. Hall said this happened:

"We hadn't been in Paris two hours until one of our boys came running, stuttering and all out of breath. He had cut an advertisement from the newspaper.

"'Look, fellows, look, great stuff! Woman wants to sell a lion cub. Let's buy it for the Escadrille. Mascot, good luck, lion cub, doctor's wife.'

"'Christamighty,' said Lufbery, 'don't be a damned fool! What would we do with a bloody lion cub! Why, grow up, don't be a continual ass!'

"'No, Luf. A lion is lucky, and we can get this one cheap!'

"No form of argument would prevent him from dragging us out to the far side of northern Paris to visit the

doctor's wife. The lion cub had been born on the Mediterra-
nean Sea . . . [and was] en route to a zoo in western France.
The moment we saw the baby lion, we fell for him. He was
a him, with blue eyes, and the most adorable manner. He
cost us 125 francs. [The equivalent of thirty dollars.] We
named him on the spot, 'Whiskey.'"

Ned Parsons described Whiskey, and his first days with
his new owners:

"He was a cute, bright-eyed baby who tried to roar in
a most ferocious manner, but who was blissfully content
the moment one gave him a finger to suck . . . Whiskey got
a splendid view of Paris during the first days he was there,
for someone in the crowd was always borrowing him to
take him some place. When it was suggested that he would
eventually have to be caged, Jim McConnell, the eloquent
pilot from Chicago who wrote the book titled *Flying for
France,* popped up with the classic remark:

"'Why put him behind bars? He'll see all the bars he
needs, traveling with this crowd.'

"So, during all the existence of the Escadrille, Whiskey
was rarely confined, but roamed at large and romped with
the pilots just like a big dog. Dogs for a long time were
his constant companions, and Luf used to say that was one
reason why Whiskey was so gentle—'Because he didn't
know he was a lion and thought he was just another dog.'

". . . When Whiskey was a year old, we figured that it
was only proper that he should have a wife, so after diligent
search we found a little female, who quite naturally was
promptly named Soda. Whiskey was tickled as a kid with a
new fire engine when he was introduced, and they got along

Fig 14. Lufbery playing with the squadron mascot Whiskey. The two became inseparable.

famously, but Soda was never the pal with us that Whiskey was. She tried to imitate him in everything he did, except his friendly attitude. She had a mean disposition, always spitting, clawing, and scratching, and never wanted to be fondled like Whiskey, who adored petting."

The fame of the mascots grew swiftly; referring to the Western Front, one of the pilots soon said, "They are known from one end of the line to the other."

Whiskey developed a great affection for Lufbery, and as he grew to full size Luf trained him to do some unconventional things. Bert Hall described that:

"One trick the two performed together was for Lufbery to plant Whiskey in ambush against some unsuspecting poilu who had been visiting the squadron for the purpose of viewing the mascots. On Lufbery's command, the lion would bound from his hiding place and pounce on the terrified visitor, usually driving the unfortunate soldier to the ground, whereupon Whiskey would put his head back and open his mouth wide, showing all his yellowed fangs in a silent laugh."

On July 14, 1915, France's great holiday of Bastille Day, the men of the *Escadrille Americaine,* yet to be renamed the Lafayette Escadrille, had a wild party at Bar-le-Duc. Their guest of honor, a twenty-two-year-old French pilot equal to any amount of celebrating, was Sous-Lieutenant Charles Nungesser. Of France's several great aces, he was the most colorful.

Nungesser's story was the stuff of legend. As his name, gold forelock, glittering blue eyes, and fair complexion

Fig 15. Whiskey and his later-acquired partner "Soda."

Fig 16. Charles Nungesser, the most colorful of the great French aces.
A handsome, party-loving man who shot down forty-five enemy planes,
twice during the war he flew for a time as a pilot attached to the Escadrille.
   His medical record was astonishing. He was wounded more than
twenty times. When a French general asked him how he had managed to
bring down so many enemy planes and survive, he replied that when he
was behind an opponent and opened fire, he closed his eyes, and when he
opened them again, sometimes he saw the German going down in flames,
"and at other times I find myself in a hospital bed."

indicated, this handsome French youth was the descendant
of Viking warriors. At sixteen, he was a well-built, fero-
ciously competitive young athlete who stood five-nine and
weighed 150 pounds. His adventurous spirit led him to set
off in 1908 for South America, where he soon found himself penniless in Buenos Aires. Hoping that his trade school
training as a mechanic might produce a job, he went to an

airfield and asked a French pilot he found there who had just landed in a Blériot monoplane, "Can I fly that?" The man replied with the French equivalent of "Get lost, kid" and walked off without looking back. Nungesser climbed into the plane, somehow got it to take off, and then made a nearly fatal landing. In those moments he fell in love with being up in the sky, and soon prevailed on a German pilot to give him flying lessons.

When Nungesser found a job in an automobile assembly plant, the company tried him out as a race car driver, and he was soon winning cash prizes in races held in Buenos Aires on Sundays. In his spare time he engaged in strenuous workouts and attended prizefights.

At one of these fights, when a French boxer was knocked out in the first round, the winner, a popular Argentine, made an impromptu speech to the crowd in which he said, "But as we know, Frenchmen are sheep who don't like to fight in the first place." Before anyone realized what was happening, Nungesser had stripped to the waist and was in the ring, getting the startled referee's permission to take off the gloves of the loser, who was still prone on the canvas, and lace them on his own fists. He faced off against the Argentine, who was thirty pounds heavier and had a far longer reach, and said, "All right, let's see you try *this* sheep." After being knocked flat twice, Nungesser put all of his 150 pounds into a short, lethal left that hit the bigger man in the solar plexus and leveled "the mastodon, who fell to the deck rolling in pain until the final count."

When France went to war in 1914, Charles Nungesser took a ship back to France and entered the fighting as a foot soldier in a fluid situation in a sector of the Western Front where trenches had not yet been dug. In one two-hour period, he fought in a skirmish during which he carried a wounded officer to safety. Then he encountered a German staff car that had become lost in the confusing wooded landscape. He drew a pistol and killed its occupants: a German colonel, a German lieutenant, and two German enlisted men. Nungesser leapt behind the wheel and delivered the car and its dead occupants to a division headquarters, where it was discovered that some papers in the car contained important military intelligence information.

Nungesser transferred to French aviation. First serving as a bomber pilot, he quickly received authorization to fly by himself wherever he pleased, night or day. Stationed on the coast, he flew fifty-three missions, bombing U-boat pens at Ostend and Zeebrugge as well as fuel and ammunition dumps and railroad yards. He returned from one mission with his plane badly damaged by enemy fire. Stepping out of the cockpit, he discovered that the toe of one of his flying boots had been shot off, but had left his foot unharmed. Even in his slow-moving bomber, on two occasions he sneaked up on swift and maneuverable German fighters and shot them down.

Sent to a fighter squadron, he shot down seven enemy planes before being asked if he would become the test pilot at the front for a new type of pursuit plane called a Ponnier. It crashed immediately upon takeoff. At the hospital the doctors found that both of his legs were broken, his jaw was smashed in such a way that it was hanging open, and most of his teeth had been knocked out. He had fragments of bullets in his lips, and blood from internal injuries oozed from his mouth.

Three days later, Charles Nungesser started making his way around the hospital on crutches, and less than a month after that he hobbled out to the flight line to try to fly again. The assembled mechanics looked at what they could see of his deathly pale face in the gaps between bandages and saw the way his jaws, now wired up but with gold teeth, glittered when he smiled. They thought he was crazy to attempt to fly in his present condition, and told him so. He replied, "Shut up and lift me into the cockpit."

Exactly two months after his accident, Nungesser started flying with the Americans of the Escadrille. He cut a flamboyant figure, wearing a special black uniform with a tight-fitting, high-collared tunic and brilliantly shined black riding boots. On his chest he had the *Légion d'Honneur,* the *Médaille Militaire,* and the *Croix de Guerre,* the latter with several palms indicating participation in different battles and campaigns. He had his mechanic paint a unique personal insignia on both sides of his plane's fuselage: a large black heart, inside of which was a white coffin above two white candles. Below that was a skull and crossbones.

Of all his dogfights, one haunted him. Attacking a German two-seater Albatros, his bullets killed the pilot, who slumped over his control stick. As the plane started a long plunge to the ground, ". . . the observer, still alive, clung desperately to the mounting ring to which his machine gun was attached. Suddenly the mounting ring ripped loose from the fuselage, and was flung into space, taking with it the hapless crewman. He clawed frantically at the air, his body working convulsively like a man on a trapeze. I had a quick glimpse of his face before he tumbled away through the clouds . . . it was a mask of horror."

While living and flying with the Escadrille, Nungesser shot down his tenth German plane. One pilot described him with these words: "A wonderful chap, blond and handsome, blue eyes, and rather square, clean-cut face; slightly sandy mustache; a striking feature is his smile which reveals two solid rows of gold teeth. He has lost his own teeth and wears a silver jaw; also walks with a limp—his left leg a little out of kilter."

Nungesser's aggressive attacking style was not lost on the Americans. They understood, appreciated, and often emulated it, and marveled at the way in which he survived frequent crashes. He served with the Escadrille twice during a combat career in which he shot down forty-five enemy planes and survived the war. In 1918, after four years of fighting, he could still keep up his dazzling, relentless attacks. On June 13 of the war's final year, he shot down two three-seater German planes in four seconds. On August 15, before breakfast, he dove through German antiaircraft fire to destroy two enemy observation balloons, and after lunch he sent two more down in flames.

His medical record astonished those who read it:

Skull fracture, brain concussion, internal injuries (multiple), five fractures of upper jaw, two fractures of lower jaw, piece of antiaircraft shrapnel embedded in right arm, dislocation of knees (left and right), re-dislocation of left knee, bullet wound in mouth, bullet wound in ear, atrophy of tendons in left leg, atrophy of muscles in calf, dislocated clavicle, dislocated wrist, dislocated right ankle, loss of teeth, contusions too numerous to mention.

Near the end of the war, the French general Robert Nivelle asked Nungesser, "Lieutenant, can you tell me by what miracle of tactics you have managed to bring down so many of the Boche?"

Nungesser replied, "Mon general, when I am behind the adversary and believe that I have his airplane well and truly centered in front of my machine guns, I close my eyes and open fire. When I open them again, sometimes I see my opponent hurtling though space . . . and at other times I find myself in a hospital bed."

Sixteen

A Bloody Report Card

As the pilots on both sides participated in increasing numbers of dogfights, they tried to record their thoughts about the instincts and actions that produced the most kills. The Allied airmen relied on anecdotal evidence, while the Germans tried a more analytical approach. All of them found no correlation between those instant reactions and previous formal education. In the memoirs of Lafayette Escadrille pilots, two of them went out of their way to say that in an aerial duel a lot of learning was a handicap. Bert Hall wrote: "From what I have observed in air fighting, I believe that the rapid decisive attack is the thing that won oftenest in the long run. Nungesser, [Georges] Guynemer, [René] Dorme, [Alfred] Heurtaux, [Albert] Deullin [the great French aces]—I have seen them all in action, and I am forced to admit that combating around one's antagonist is a very dull and exasperating procedure, compared with the quick dive, fire, and pull-away method . . . it's a victory or you go down afire. For, if you live to pull away at all, you must have pulled away with everything you had . . . Nerve and a heavy hand are what decided most air battles."

Ned Parsons was even more specific. "It seemed to us on the front, where only the fittest or the luckiest survived, that a . . . man capable of handling a ship well and shooting straight, was worth ten mediocre fliers with college degrees . . . Ability, courage, and a cool head appeared to be the best qualifications. Oft-times too much knowledge was filled with danger and defeated its own ends, for it led to too much imagination, the ruination of many a splendid young war bird."

A British pilot weighed in with this: "Like dueling, air fighting required a set, steely courage, drained of all emotion, fined down to a tense and deadly effort of will. The Angel of Death is less callous, aloof, and implacable than a fighting pilot when he dives."

In a sense, the Germans attempted to start their analysis before the war began. In the years before 1914, the Germans made many plans for the aerial side of a potential war. The German General Staff, all stern Prussians, foresaw that victorious pilots would become national heroes. They went to great lengths to identify and develop the men they thought would be aces. As the war continued, the High Command kept meticulous records of how their pilots performed, and their accounts of what they did and felt.

Ironically, the first of their best pilots was not a Prussian like von Richthofen or Richthofen's mentor, Oswald Boelcke, but a cheerful, gentle Bavarian, an eighteen-year-old from Munich who was initially rejected because he was only five-foot-three, an inch below the physical requirement that German pilots be at least five-four. This was Ernst Udet, a lad who had always been crazy about airplanes. He tried to enlist on August 2, 1914, the day after Germany began the four-year bloodbath by declaring war on Russia. After several more attempts to join up, Ernst discovered that if he could get a civilian pilot's license, he would immediately be accepted as a pilot in the German Army Air Service, no matter how short he was. He received private tutoring through a family friend who owned an aircraft factory—flying lessons that cost a total of 2,000 marks, worth about 420 American dollars at the time.

His early months as a pilot showed no sign of brilliance, although he and an observer managed to improvise a landing of a two-seater after a shackle on the cable that held a wing to the plane broke off in mid-flight. Next, flying a two-seater loaded with too much fuel and too many bombs, he stalled out and had a crash landing in which his astonishing luck first demonstrated itself: Neither the fuel nor the bombs exploded. He was court-martialed for negligence for not realizing that the plane could not fly effectively while carrying so much weight, and spent seven days in the guardhouse.

Udet's career then took turns for the better and worse. Flying another two-seater from which his observer threw a small bomb that became stuck in the landing gear, he managed to perform some acrobatic maneuvers that shook the bomb loose. That feat earned him a transfer to a squadron of new single-seater Fokker fighter planes. In his first opportunity to shoot down an enemy plane, he slipped in behind a French Caudron, lined it up in his sights, and found he "could not bring himself to pull the trigger." As a result, the French pilot swung around and riddled Udet's plane with machine gun fire. One bullet sliced open his cheek and shattered his goggles, but he was still able to land his plane.

That encounter changed Ernst Udet. In his next combat mission, while on standby, he was ordered to "scramble" his aircraft, take off swiftly, and intercept what were reported to be two British planes headed toward his squadron's base. Instead, as he reached altitude he found more than twenty enemy aircraft, bombers with fighters protecting them. Attacking a Farman two-seat bomber, as he pulled away he saw the plane catch fire and the observer fall out of the rear seat. He described the moment: "The fuselage of the Farman dives down past me like a giant torch . . . A man, his arms and legs spread out like a frog's, falls past—the observer. At the moment, I don't think of them as human beings. I only feel one thing—victory, triumph, victory!"

In the next few months Ernst brought down five more planes, becoming an ace, and then was assigned to elite fighter squadrons, in which he shot down nine more planes. At the age of twenty-one he became a squadron commander, evaluated this way in a biography of him published eighty-nine years later: "Despite his seemingly frivolous nature, drinking late into the night and womanizing, he proved an excellent squadron commander. He spent many hours coaching neophyte fighter pilots, with an emphasis on marksmanship as being essential for success."

A supreme accolade awaited him. On a day of torrential rain in Flanders, he was struggling to pitch a tent in

Fig 17. In a little-known picture, von Richthofen lines up his "Flying Circus" to be presented to the Kaiser. The photograph is illustrative of the German discipline that made their squadrons so effective in the air. No group of Allied airmen ever turned out with such a parade-ground appearance.

the mud when a staff car drove up, splashing through deep puddles. Out stepped Baron Manfred von Richthofen, the most famous of the German aces. At the age of twenty-five he commanded a fighter group of four squadrons (forty-eight planes) and had the authority to invite any German pilot to join his "Flying Circus." He told Udet that he knew of his twenty kills, and said, "You would actually seem ripe for us. Would you like to?" Standing there in the mud, twenty-one-year-old Ernst Udet accepted the invitation to join the Flying Circus on the spot.

*   *   *

When the American pilots of the newly organized Escadrille encountered men like Richthofen, Boelcke, and Udet, it was a near-miracle that any of them survived. To start flying against these German aces during the furious Battle of Verdun could only be seen as a stupendous mismatch. After two years of aerial warfare the Germans were on their way to an overall wartime record of having more than three hundred pilots who became aces.

The German fighter pilots received better training from the start. Compared with the three-month advanced training the French gave their own fighter pilots and the Americans who flew for them, the Germans were tutored for twice that time by some of the best German pilots. When one adds the French statistic that the average life expectancy of a fighter pilot in combat was fifteen hours in the air, the only explanation for the Escadrille's survival rate appears to be the innate skill and courage of its pilots.

Seventeen

Bert Hall as Thinker, Bartender, and Raconteur

While being an ultimate man of action, Bert Hall also did some thinking. He sensed and recorded the dehumanizing effects of months of combat, and wrote:

"Saw two French pilots buried yesterday. They decorated the graves with the remains of the smashed airplane. Personally, I think this business of displaying the remains of airplanes on the graves of dead pilots is very bad. It's bad for the troops. Half burned or otherwise demolished remains of airplanes belong on the junk heap, and if I had my way, that's where they would land."

Hall, who in one dogfight had a German bullet enter the right side of his mouth, knock out several of his teeth, and leave through the left side of his neck, had another experience that few pilots had. During a dogfight he poured machine gun fire into a new type of German fighter plane called a Pfalz, and saw it land on a British base. He followed it down and landed near it "to see if any of the nice new Pfalz was fit to take back for examination."

Once out of his plane, he saw that the enemy pilot was badly wounded. "They had him sitting on the ground beside the remains of a smashed-up building. I've only seen a few of my victims, and I'm sorry I saw this one. He had an awful look on his face. It was more like a female animal going through an abortive birth than anything I ever saw in my life. He couldn't talk but the Intelligence Officers were examining his papers and finding out everything they could. But the death look on that Boche's face was enough to take the swank out of me."

Living amid pilots who drank a lot, Bert drank little, but provided some alcoholic sustenance for his friends. At the time, a cocktail known as a Manhattan was a great favorite among relatively sophisticated drinkers. It was made of whiskey, vermouth, and often a dash of bitters. Among those who preferred it were Bill Thaw and Lufbery. Using a metal pail, Bert would mix up a good quantity of the drink, then watch his friends go to work on it.

Especially with Thaw, this seemed to seal an already strong friendship. Thaw saw Bert Hall as a man who told some tall tales, but Bert always believed that Thaw had saved his life in one of the Escadrille's early battles. As he remembered it, a German fighter plane was coming right at him from the side, about to open fire, when Thaw, coming out of nowhere, appeared between them and took a burst from the German's machine guns that Bert thought would have killed him. Thaw was badly wounded in his shoulder and right elbow, with the result that he could never stretch his right arm to its full length again, but he went on to become a fine leader. Interestingly, among several wounds that Hall received during the war, one he suffered on June 26, 1917, was similar to the one Thaw sustained. Writing in 1918, he said, "With me the great trouble is that my right arm doesn't work the way it used to, but it is getting into fair shape again. The doctors have built up the part from the shoulder to the elbow so that it looks like an arm again."

As a raconteur, Hall had a talent for describing raucous situations. At one point, when the Escadrille had again been stationed on one side of the Luxeuil airfield and British bombers of the Royal Naval Air Force were stationed on the other, the Escadrille was grounded because the pilots had flown there, but their mechanics, traveling by land, had not caught up to them.

"One afternoon an English officer came to us and said: 'Say, you bloomin' Yanks, let's call the war off and celebrate.' So we invited them to dinner down at the Hotel Lion d'Or. Everything went on beautifully until the 'binge' began, and then there was a tendency to throw plates—just playful like—now a plate and now a saucer. The management of the Lion d'Or got worried, but it was no use. No amount of worrying could have saved the dishes. Before the party ended all the moveable equipment was a washout.

"Next morning as soon as we were all together we decided to do a good job on the Britishers' equipment at the very next opportunity. We didn't have to wait long . . . By noontime, a message came from the British C.O., inviting us to their mess that evening. 'Ah, ha,' said Lufbery. 'Now we get even with the Limeys.'

"I couldn't begin to tell you the things that happened at that celebration. We called off the war and went at it. At first, the British Commanding Officer proposed toasts to the King and to President Poincaré and to President Wilson and a lot of folks. And then he made a short speech. Captain Thenault responded in very good English and that ended the civilities . . . The Britishers knew we were going to do wrong by them but they didn't know when or how.

"When the time came I never knew who gave the signal, but the carnage was terrible. The chairs, the tables, the dishes, the bottles, everything went before the energy of our attack . . . When we started, the [British] barracks was divided up by many little partitions. When we finished it was all one big room. God, it was wonderful!—the ripping and crashing of the lumber and the complete devastation of the cots and the other equipment. The Britishers didn't mind at all; as a matter of fact, I once saw the British Major and Captain Thenault laughing as if they would explode and drinking each other's health over and over again.

"Just before the celebration was said to be over, we heard some shots outside. We looked out and there to our astonishment was a tall Canadian from Vancouver shooting at a book. The book was being held at arm's length by none other than Raoul Lufbery. The Canadian had been a member of the Northwestern Mounted Police. He could shoot too, because he was hitting the book every time, in spite of Lufbery's unsteady target.

"The British Major stopped the target practice. Inside, we examined the book. It was a thin volume of British drill regulations. The Canadian sharpshooter gave us each a page from the book as a souvenir of the evening. The pages were perforated with five jagged holes.

"When at last we started home . . . the Royal Naval Air Force declared in a body that we were the best gang of Yanks they had ever encountered. 'We didn't expect you blighters would be 'arf so sociable, you know,' one of the pilots said. 'Not 'arf.'"

Eighteen

Bad Things Happen to Good New Men

Good men kept coming into the Escadrille. One of the later arrivals was Harold Willis of Boston, born in 1890, who had played on Harvard's championship football team. In 1914 he gave up his practice as a promising young architect and sailed for France to serve in one of the ambulance units run by the American Field Service. He received the French *Croix de Guerre* with silver star for going far beyond his duties as an ambulance driver when he crawled out on a battlefield to drag wounded men to safety. Willis described his time as a driver on the Western Front: "Two of the best years of my life with that magnificent creature, the rank-and-file Frenchman during his most heroic moments."

By 1916 Willis felt he should take an even more active role in the war, and in effect deserted from his ambulance unit, and went to Paris. He enlisted in the Foreign Legion on June 1 of 1916 and within a month transferred to the French Air Service. After months of training, on March 1 of 1917 he arrived at Ravenel, ninety-five miles north of Paris, where the Escadrille was spending the winter in a place where the mud was often so thick and frozen that the planes could not take off.

Things were as bad at Ham, thirty-five miles to the east, to which the squadron moved on April 7. Willis described it as a "pretty dismal world . . . The Germans had blown up all railroads and all crossroads. They had cut down all the fruit trees and poisoned all the wells."

Despite the terrible conditions on the ground and in the air, Willis settled in well, and he and Edward Hinkle, another architect and at forty-one the oldest man in the Escadrille, designed the squadron's Indian Head insignia. What emerged was the profile of a ferocious Sioux brave wearing his red-white-and-blue feathered bonnet, which was painted on the fuselage of all the Escadrille's planes.

While he was getting acquainted with the overall sector of operations, Willis made himself useful to the unit by dropping in at different towns well behind the lines that were known for the good wines grown in their areas. He would pick up a dozen or more bottles of a good vintage, and bring them back to brighten up an evening in the squadron mess.

Willis also furthered his own architectural interests. Ned Parsons remembered a day when Willis was overdue for more than an hour after his squadron mates returned from a mission in the skies over Compiègne. There was a growing feeling that something bad had befallen him. Just then Willis showed up, making an uneventful landing. Asked about his delay in getting back, as one pilot recalled it,

Willis answered that he had decided "to fly to Chartres—nearly a hundred miles to the south—to get an aerial view of the cathedral there. He walked across the field to the barracks to warm up, still expounding on the glories of Gothic architecture."

Then Willis made himself more militarily useful.

"I tried photographic work with a [single-seater] SPAD. The French were very interested in it because I could go deep into the [enemy] lines very quickly. I took stereoscopic pictures by flying at a given altitude and a given speed and taking pictures by a stop watch."

Captain Thenault was impressed by what Willis could do.

"With his trained and intelligent brain he always brought back from trips information that was greatly prized by the High Command. It is very hard to take good observations from a single-seater. Willis had made a specialty of it and thanks to the speed of his machine, he was able to go to places here the slower two-seaters could not have ventured without being brought down."

While Willis was flying a dawn patrol mission behind German lines at Verdun on August 18, 1916, his engine was destroyed by machine gun fire from a German fighter pilot. As Willis glided down over German territory, looking for a place to land, he experienced this: "The German pilot shot up my windshield and he finally shot my glasses [goggles] off, which was close enough. When Willis landed, "This German who shot me down landed right behind me, which was good luck, because a group of German soldiers came running up, and he was able to protect me. Sometimes [captured] pilots were badly treated by soldiers on both sides . . . This pilot who shot me down proved to be completely correct and considerate. We waited around and pretty soon some other officers came up in a car and we all went down to the German pilot's own field and had breakfast together." At breakfast, when Willis struggled out of his one-piece flying suit, his German hosts were startled to find that he was wearing only a pair of green striped pajama trousers and two oil-stained sweaters.

Back at their home base, Ned Parsons, alert as always, used this to Willis's advantage. Packing up some of Willis's possessions he intended to drop behind enemy lines in the hope they would ultimately reach Willis, he realized that, because Willis had not flown that day wearing his uniform tunic, which would have identified him as being a sergeant, he could address the package to "Lieutenant Harold Willis"—"thus assuring him better treatment as an officer." (Willis had also identified himself as being an officer, and the deception lasted for months.)

Later on the day he was shot down, Willis was taken to what he described as "an old medieval prison with a lot of French officers." A man posing as a fellow prisoner, wearing "a dirty French Officer's uniform," tried "to become very friendly and asked a great many questions concerning the disposition of Allied forces." Willis correctly deduced that he was a German intelligence officer "and no information was given." He was there for the better part of a month, before being moved on to what proved to be a succession of prison camps, and recalled his frame of mind:

"I wasn't very proud of being a prisoner. In prison one has the feeling that perhaps if he had put up a better fight he wouldn't have been taken. The only way to clear one's self of that feeling was to damned well escape. I did, eventually, quite a long time afterwards."

What Willis did not mention in that brief account was that he made several attempts to escape. In his efforts to do so, he and some accomplices received no help from the West Pointers who were imprisoned with them. In his first attempt, made in mid-March of 1918, he reached the outer barbed wire of a prisoner-of-war camp at Lübeck, a German port city on the Baltic Sea thirty-six miles northeast of Hamburg. He was recaptured trying to get through the wire, and sent to the first of two camps deeper into Germany. In the second camp, Villingen in the Black Forest region near the Swiss border, Willis lived in the worst conditions he had experienced since his capture eleven months before. The camp consisted of a "pen of huts" with a virtually complete lack of sanitary facilities. Willis said of the place, "The whole place is alive with fleas and vermin of all sorts."

The vile camp had two redeeming features. Perhaps because of its proximity to the Swiss border, Red Cross packages of food arrived there with some regularity, keeping Willis and his fellow prisoners from starving.

The second thing was the presence of Lieutenant Victor M. Isaacs of the United States Navy, whose ship had been sunk by a German submarine off the French coast. Isaacs was the only American naval officer captured by the Germans during the war. He and Willis escaped together, finally crossing into neutral Switzerland by swimming across the freezing-cold Rhine River at night and getting back to Paris shortly before the war ended.

Willis returned to Boston and his successful career as an architect, but he and France had another war ahead of them. In 1940, then aged fifty, Willis was once again wearing the uniform of the American Field Service, and driving an ambulance as he had at the beginning of the First World War. When France fell, Willis escaped into Spain just ahead of the Germans, and ended up in the United States Army Air Force, serving in North Africa on the staff of General Carl A. "Tooey" Spaatz's Twelfth Air Force as chief tactical officer holding the rank of colonel. After World War Two he again resumed his practice as an architect, joining the firm Allen & Collens of Boston. Among the buildings they designed are the Riverside Church and Union Theological Seminary in Manhattan, and several at Mount Holyoke College.

Nineteen

Convenient Emergencies

Paris was the greatly preferred destination for any flier given even a short leave, but the members of the Escadrille came to realize that there was another way of getting a night or two away from the squadron. Engines had a way of sometimes sputtering or ceasing to function altogether. From high in the air a pilot would try to glide down and make a forced landing inside his own lines, and as he did that he would look for a handsome château surrounded by flat grassy pastures.

As the air war began, a stranded pilot would send a message back to his airfield, sometimes by telephone, saying where he was, and asking that the squadron send a staff car and a couple of mechanics to repair his plane so that he could fly it back. Often this required a stay of two or three days, and the pilot would return with a big smile and a report of splendid hospitality at the home of the Baron This or the Countess That. The host might have had an exceptional chef, the château might possess marvelous baths and soft beds, and some families had charming daughters who were happy to spend evenings with that novelty, an American who dropped from the sky.

It was not long before the Escadrille's commander, Captain Thenault, began to understand that some of these mechanical breakdowns were not always what they seemed. On the other hand, they appeared to be good for the men's morale, and as long as a pilot did not report this kind of emergency too often, another man would fly in his place the next day, knowing that the favor would be returned.

One day Ned Parsons found himself in a genuine emergency, in which his electrical system "just cut out for good and all." He glided down into "the park of a château," overshot the flat area, "and went into the underbrush and trees on the other side in a grand crash." He found himself "hanging head down about seven or eight feet off the ground, and all my weight was on my safety belt." A peasant came around under the upside-down plane, looked up, and asked in French if he could help. Using his limited French vocabulary, Parsons explained to the man how he could help by pushing him up until his weight was off the belt's clasp so that he could release it.

"He pushed up all right, but as soon as I cracked the belt he hastily ducked from under and let me drop squarely on the back of my neck. It . . . knocked me out for fifteen minutes.

"I awoke with my head in the lap of a charming and very beautiful English girl, whose husband, a French officer at the front, owned the château.

"I was there for several days till the wrecking crew came. Then they had two wrecks to take care of. I was the other."

Bert Hall found a different way to spend some time away from the squadron. Writing an account of his activities, he said:

"That was a great gag I worked on the French authorities, and it lengthened out my leave five days. Originally, I was supposed to have only one day, but Lufbery put me onto a good one and I worked it to a standstill. You see, the French Intelligence Department knows that I have traveled all over the world and have spent a lot of time in Germany, so when I called one of their operators on the telephone and told him that I had just seen a German officer dressed up like a middle-aged French business man, they took the bait, hook, line and sinker.

"They proposed that they supply me with a shadowing expert and let both of us get on with the job, but I discouraged the idea. All I needed was time and a little cash. The Headquarters supplied both of these commodities and for six days, I did all the cafes and restaurants in Paris looking for my fugitive."

Hall's friends in the squadron also thought that his caper in Paris, suggested by Lufbery, was "a great gag," but some of the newer pilots felt with some reason that Hall's absence from the flying roster increased their own chances of being killed or wounded. In time, that resentment would grow.

Twenty

Unique Volunteers

Two Americans who took to the French skies in 1916 could not have come from more different backgrounds. The first was Kenneth Marr of Oakland, California. In 1908, then eighteen, he went to Nome, Alaska. By 1914 he and a partner named Scotty Allen were in the business of raising huskies and training and performing with a team of those sled dogs.

When the war began, Marr's enterprising partner contracted with the French government to supply three hundred huskies for dog sled teams to evacuate wounded French *Chasseurs Alpins* [mountain troops] from the often snow-covered Vosges Mountains on the Swiss end of the Western Front. Marr, accompanied by two Alaskan dog-handling Indians, delivered the sled dogs to France. Finding himself on the edge of a rapidly expanding conflict, Marr entered the American Field Service as an ambulance driver, was gassed at Verdun, and spent a brief period in the Foreign

Legion. In late July of 1916 he transferred to the French Air Service, and began a long period of training that ended with his being assigned to the Lafayette Escadrille in early January of 1917, three months before the United States entered the war. His squadron mates nicknamed him "Si" because of his association with the two Alaskan tribesmen, sometimes known as Siwash Indians.

Marr had what could be called either good luck or bad. On a morning soon after joining the Escadrille, he was scheduled to take off on an early patrol with four more experienced pilots. Those four had problems with their planes that stopped them from taking off. Marr got into the air, and quickly found his engine sputtering and cutting out. Circling back to the field to land, as he came in to touch down he hit some twisted railroad tracks at the end of a grassy airstrip. His plane flipped on its back and slid down an embankment, ending up as a shattered skeleton. Marr emerged with nothing more than bruises, and began to show some of the determination and courage that characterized the sled dogs he had worked with for years.

In Marr's next brush with fate, after shooting down a German Albatros scout plane, a week later he found himself, now flying a SPAD, being attacked by two enemy fighters. He disabled one of them, but the other German stayed right on his tail, firing his machine guns until the bullets cut through the cables that controlled Marr's ability to use the flaps on his wings to climb or descend. Even after one of his squadron mates drove off this second German, Marr was flying at an altitude of six thousand feet without being able to use any of the usual controls.

Ingeniously, he used his throttle, speeding up and slowing down, working his plane the vertical distance of more than a mile down to the ground in a safe landing among a grove of trees in the Hesse Forest. Then he leapt from his plane and jumped into a staff car whose occupants had been waiting to see if he would come down alive. Thinking quickly, he had the driver cut through the woods to his home field, where he picked up a mechanic and a length of cable. Returning to his shot-up plane, he replaced everything that had been severed by German bullets, and got his SPAD back in the air. He flew it back to his field, refueled, and set off on another patrol.

In his next memorable encounter, some weeks later, Marr single-handedly managed to hold off *six* German fighters that were attacking an Allied photo plane, maneuvering and firing to protect it until it reached friendly lines. He then turned and went back into enemy territory. Spotting a German two-seater, he dove at it from behind, coming out of the sun and getting within fifty yards of its tail before firing twenty rounds at it. This killed the pilot, but the backward-facing observer stood up behind his twin machine guns and blasted right back at Marr, who had this reaction:

"I certainly felt sorry for the helpless beggar. There he was dashing to a certain death but to the last gamely trying to give me a fight." The enemy plane "dived steeply, turning sideways, and banged into the ground about three miles inside Germany."

*   *   *

When the United States came into the war, Marr was one of the pilots who elected to fly with an American squadron. He ended up as a captain commanding the famous 94th "Hat in the Ring" Pursuit Squadron, later to be led by Eddie Rickenbacker, who emerged from the war as the leading American ace. Rickenbacker, a lieutenant already serving with the unit, wrote an account of what could have been the last minutes of Marr's life. Not seeing each other, Marr and a Lieutenant Thorne Taylor landed at opposite ends of a long grass airstrip at Toul, then ran into each other, getting their wings tangled up while their engines continued to roar, and, as Rickenbacker described it, spinning "around and around . . . like a top."

That was dangerous enough, but the collision had knocked loose Marr's machine gun in a way that started it firing as the plane continued to spin, sending 650 bullets a minute across the field like "a gigantic pin wheel shooting out living sparks in every direction." Military personnel of every sort dove for cover; miraculously, no one was hurt.

Evidently the incident was not held against either pilot. In due course Marr was promoted to major, decorated by both the French and American armies, and with the Armistice returned to the United States. He finished his military service in 1919 as the commander of an aerial gunnery school near San Diego. This brought him back at the age of twenty-nine to his native California, which he had left to go to Alaska eleven action-packed years before.

Marr went on to lead one of the most interesting and productive postwar lives of any Escadrille pilot. Hollywood

FIRST TO FLY   153

was just emerging as the nation's movie capital. Hiring on at Paramount Pictures, he became an assistant to the legendary director John Ford, who was starting a career that would bring him six Oscars. It was there that Marr met the silent screen actress Alice Ward, and they married in 1928.

Soon after that, Kenneth Marr switched his talents and energy to an entirely different kind of business. He started the Marr and Janeway Company, which began drilling successfully for oil in areas where old oil leases had expired. Creating something of a conglomerate, he took a substantial amount of his oil profits and began buying timberland and other real estate, including a five-thousnd-acre sheep ranch in Humboldt County, California. After several years of comfortable retirement in Phoenix, Arizona, he died in Palo Alto, California, in 1963 at the age of seventy-eight. He had lived a uniquely American success story—a boy who went into the world and became a decorated fighter pilot, a Hollywood figure, an oilman, and a rancher, married to a movie star.

The second one-of-a-kind American flier to take to the skies of France in 1916 was Eugene Bullard, who would become the first black American fighter pilot. Born in 1895 in Columbus, Georgia, as a boy Eugene experienced hardship as well as incidents of violent racial prejudice, mixed with kindness from white families. His father, William, was a big, exceptionally strong man, part Creek Indian, who lived by a code that Eugene could still recite when he was sixty-six years old:

"I want you all to be good children. Always show respect to everyone, white and black, and make them respect you. Go to school as long as you can. Never look for a fight. I mean never. But if you are attacked, or your honor is attacked unjust [sic], fight, fight, keep on fighting even if you die for your rights. It will be a glorious death."

Eugene left home with $1.50 in his pocket at the age of twelve, and soon fell in with a band of gypsies. From them, he first heard of places across the Atlantic like France, where an African-American could expect better treatment than he or she would receive in the United States. In the next four years of his adolescence, he worked his way as a day laborer across Georgia, sometimes hitchhiking or slipping aboard freight trains. Eventually he came to Richmond, Virginia, and went on to Norfolk. By the time he was sixteen, he had filled out physically, and had developed a strong sense of financial responsibility and personal safety—although he would sleep in the barns or in the houses of those who employed him, he had a fear of being picked up as a vagrant. He kept a little ledger in which he made scores of entries showing that, rather than sleeping in public places such as a park, he often paid for a room for the night.

On the docks at Newport News he befriended members of the German crew of the *Marta Russ,* a two-thousand-ton freighter about to begin a three-week crossing of the Atlantic to the Scottish port of Aberdeen. The seamen enabled him to become a stowaway, but the captain soon learned of his presence aboard, and put him to work in the boiler room. When the vessel reached Aberdeen, Captain Westphal paid him five pounds and sent him ashore at night in a rowboat to avoid any complications Eugene might encounter with the port authorities.

Eugene Bullard began reinventing himself. First he made his way from Aberdeen to Glasgow, and then on to Liverpool. At an amusement park he saw a sideshow at which customers paid to throw soft rubber balls at a person's head that stuck up through a black sheet. Eugene convinced the sideshow owner that the passersby would rather throw rubber balls at the head of a black man than a white one. He was right about that and, working only on weekends, was soon making more money than he ever had doing hard labor.

That proved to be Eugene Bullard's introduction to show business. Within months he was doing slapstick acts in vaudeville shows; one was called "Belle Davis's Freedman's Pickaninnies." In his spare time he began hanging around gymnasiums, where Aaron Lester Brown, a black American prizefighter who boxed under the name the "Dixie Kid," decided that Eugene had what it took to become one of his stable of fighters and brought him along with them to London. Bullard won a number of welterweight fights there, and the Dixie Kid arranged for him to have a bout in Paris.

It was in Paris that Bullard found the physical and emotional home of which the gypsies in Georgia had told him. He said of that discovery that he knew that "[I] could never be happy for the rest of my life unless I could live in France."

At a time when he was enjoying his new home— winning some fights, strolling the boulevards, and getting to know the museums and savoring the cuisine—the Germans declared war. By early September of 1914, the Germans were almost at the Marne, and the French government was appealing to every able-bodied man, of whatever nationality or race, to fight for France.

On October 9, 1914, Eugene Bullard's nineteenth birthday, he enlisted in the Foreign Legion. Already an athlete in excellent condition, his fitness hardened by three months of grueling training at a Legion base in Paris, by April of 1915 he was a machine gunner fighting in repeated battles along the Somme in north-central France. Surviving a year of attacks and retreats that killed hundreds of thousands of men, he suffered three minor wounds and in February of 1916 was sent to Verdun. In all this fighting he never lost his revulsion toward killing, while realizing that his increasing skill with a machine gun was saving many of his comrades. In a later oral history interview that was transcribed in a way that emphasized his black diction, he described what it was like to mow down an advancing force of German infantrymen.

"When you stopped to cool [the machine gun] and the other gun picked up the *feu* [fire], you could see 'em wriggling like worms in the bait box.

"Yassir, I was sick, awful sick! Every time the sargent yelled 'feu!' I got sicker and sicker. They had wives and children hadn't they?"

At Verdun, Eugene saw the worst scenes yet.

"The whole front seemed to be moving like a saw backwards and forwards . . . as earth was plowed under, men and beasts [hung] from the branches of trees where they had been blown to pieces." On March 5, 1916, he was hit by shrapnel from an artillery shell that cut open his thigh and knocked out several of his teeth. Despite these wounds, he carried a message under fire from one officer to another—an act for which he would receive the *Croix de Guerre* with bronze star. He then spent three months in a military hospital outside of Paris and three months of further convalescence in a private clinic in a château in the city of Lyon, in southeastern France. When Bullard fell into conversation with the commander of the French airfield at Bron, five miles from Lyon, that officer asked him what he planned to do next. Aware that he would never be able to return to the trenches, Bullard replied that with his many hours of experience with machine guns, he could probably do a good job firing a machine gun from a plane. When Bullard subsequently learned that pilots made considerably more money than the men who fired machine guns from the backseat, a friend remarked that Bullard "knew damn well that he wanted to be a pilot rather than an aviation gunner."

During a convalescent trip to Paris, Eugene was sitting in a Montparnasse café with a white Southerner named Jeff Dickson who was proud of this wounded and decorated black man who was doing so well in the war. Dickson said in a cautionary way, "You know there aren't any Negroes in aviation." Bullard replied, "Sure I do. That's why I want to get into it."

On November 15, 1916, having had help from a number of French officers, Eugene Bullard received orders to report for pilot training at Tours in the Loire Valley. He and his behind-the-scenes supporters had worked hard to make this happen, and he went on to fly more than twenty combat missions. Then orders came for him to stop flying and take a desk job at the headquarters of the French 170th Infantry

Regiment. Bewildered and disappointed, his friends discovered that this was the work of Dr. Edmund Gros, who had done so much to put American fliers into French skies. In screening applicants for the Lafayette Escadrille, Gros had established the requirement that they should not be of German descent, but it seemed that he also did not want an American pilot who was black.

This marked only the first half of Eugene Bullard's story, which would continue in Paris during the 1920s and '30s, and ended in Manhattan in October of 1961. During all those years, the gifts and strengths and fame that brought him to the sky above the Western Front would keep a remarkable cast of characters, black and white, circulating through his life.

Remaining in Paris after the war, Bullard acted as a bouncer and sometime manager at Bricktop's, a fashionable 1920s nightspot owned by the famous black American dancer known as "Bricktop." At times Bullard also owned and ran a gymnasium, and a spa. He married a French countess and they had two daughters.

Bullard had some fights in postwar Paris that did not take place in boxing rings. To his regret, he found that most of these were started by American white men who did not like to see white women of any nationality consorting with big, strong black men, and particularly not with an American black man who was famous and popular because of his record in the war. In one memorable fracas, Bullard and his old London mentor and friend the Dixie Kid were attacked by a gang of sailors at a big dance hall in Montmartre called the Olympia. Pursued by the sailors, Bullard and the Dixie

Kid dashed up a wide staircase. Turning at the top, Bullard picked up the leading sailor and threw him down the steps in such a way that the man knocked the others over like pins in a bowling alley. Then he and the Dixie Kid began a counterattack that "cleaned out the whole bunch."

Bullard remained one of the colorful figures in the Paris of the '20s and '30s, chatting with intellectuals and other celebrities, occasionally organizing jazz bands to play in concerts for worthy causes, and being friendly to anyone whose looks he liked.

When the Germans overran France in 1940, Eugene became a member of the French underground, eventually serving under the famous female Resistance leader Cleopatre Terrier. A good part of his effectiveness came from German racial philosophy: The Nazis could not believe that a member of what they saw as an *Untermenschen*—an inferior species—was intelligent enough to be a good Resistance fighter, nor that the French would entrust him with life-and-death missions. Bullard originally thought that Cleopatre was a Nazi collaborator, and she thought the same of him.

Severely wounded fighting the Nazis, Eugene was spirited out of the country and settled in New York City. In 1954 he was invited to return to France as a guest of the French government to participate in a ceremony in Paris marking the fortieth anniversary of the beginning of the First World War. Bullard, along with the two white French veterans of that war who flanked him, rekindled the Eternal Flame at the tomb of France's Unknown Soldier under the Arc de Triomphe.

Twenty-one

The War Changes Men and Women, Some for Better, and Some for Worse

At the front, a few men of the Escadrille began to fall apart. Ned Parsons had spoken of some amount of alcohol being "an absolute necessity" for the nerves of a combat pilot, but a number now drank more than what Parsons had in mind, night after night. The deaths of some may have been due to their hungover condition when they flew in combat, but a pilot named Laurence Rumsey created a different situation.

Rumsey was yet one more man from a wealthy background, a Harvard graduate from Buffalo, New York, who played professional polo before the war. Assigned to the Escadrille, when he was given his own plane he too-prophetically had a large white RUM painted on its fuselage as his personal identification.

One morning, despite his fellow pilots urging him not to fly while still befuddled by drink, Rumsey took off on a mission in which they were to take their planes to a new base. Becoming disoriented and separated from the formation in which he was supposed to fly, he finally landed at an Allied airfield he did not know. In his stupefied state he became convinced that it was a German base, and followed the instructions for what to do in that eventuality. He set his plane on fire, destroying it so that it would not fall into enemy hands.

That made him the subject of concern, but the squadron kept him on. One evening in November of 1916, when Rumsey was in the unit's little bar at Cachy in the muddy, blood-soaked Somme Valley, drinking too much brandy as usual, the squadron's mascot lion Whiskey began to play with Rumsey's braided uniform cap, holding it between his paws and chewing on it. Rumsey shouted at him to stop, and Whiskey growled as he continued to mangle the cap. Rumsey grabbed up a cane and started beating Whiskey all over the head. Whiskey dropped the cap and tottered over to a table where other pilots were playing poker. Stopping their game to look at Whiskey's battered head, they found that Rumsey had injured their mascot in his right eye. Bill Thaw took Whiskey to Paris for an examination by an eye doctor, who confirmed that Whiskey would never see out of that eye again.

The episode left Rumsey unstrung: Coupled with the fact that during his five months' service with the Escadrille he had seen three fellow pilots killed and three wounded, the episode sent him into a complete physical and mental decline. Within days he was lying in a hospital, covered with boils. After seven months' hospitalization, he was sent back to the United States, which by then was in the war. To his credit, despite his medical discharge he enlisted in the

United States Army as a private—though he was never sent overseas again—and he ended his military service in January of 1919 as a first lieutenant. After the war he resumed his polo playing with considerable success, living in upstate New York on his inherited money. He never married, and never initiated contact with surviving members of the Escadrille. In 1967, at the age of eighty, he died in his apartment in Buffalo in a room filled with prizes won in polo matches.

Escadrille pilot Charles Dolan, an observant young man, recorded two matters found nowhere else in the printed story of the Escadrille. First, he noted an overall change in sexual behavior as the war ground on.

"You couldn't walk a block in Paris without fifty girls coming up to you and saying, 'I sleep with you tonight, yes?' Everybody, anybody. The woods were full of them. We were at the Countess of Bethune's one weekend. She was having a party for the Escadrille. I asked her, why all this lack of morality. She said, 'You don't realize. See that girl over there, and this applies to most of the girls in this room.' There were about ten of them she had invited to entertain us. 'She's one of fifty in her family, and there's only four men left. Their husbands, their fathers, their brothers are all dead.'"

Dolan's second unique account involved an Escadrille pilot who was done in by his cowardice. Dolan never revealed the man's name, but said this in an interview for an oral history program conducted by the United States Air Force in 1968:

"There was one incident where this fellow would be in a patrol, and he'd fly until they crossed the [enemy] line, and then he'd drop out with engine trouble or something and come home. The next day he'd drop out because the sun had blinded him or something. At any rate he would fly along the lines. And when the squadron had come back, over the lines, he'd drop in place. This got so bad that at the end of about a month the fellows shot him down—his own men shot him down. They did not want any Frenchmen to think that they had these kinds of Americans. So he's among the missing, and his record is unnamed in the history of the Escadrille."

Strong as the ties of comradeship were among most of the Escadrille pilots, a rivalry sprang up. Sadly, it involved two of the best men in the squadron, "Founders" Norman Prince, who had helped get French approval for the Escadrille's formation, and Paul Rockwell's younger brother Kiffin. The younger Rockwell became convinced that Captain Thenault had been favoring Prince. This came to a head when Thenault credited Prince with what Rockwell thought was a questionable kill, and recommended him for the highly regarded *Médaille Militaire*. In a letter to Paul in Paris, Kiffin burst out with this: "No one thinks that X [Prince] got a German, in fact everyone is sure that he didn't; yet the Captain proposed him for a citation, wanted to propose him for the *Médaille,* but everyone said that if he did they would quit. I am going to have to call him [Prince] out when he gets back from Paris, as he talked awfully big about us behind my back while I was away. We have all agreed to try to run him out of the squadron."

As for Thenault, who went right on with his recommendation of the *Médaille Militaire* for Prince, Kiffin had this to say: "We are very unlucky in having a captain who is a nice fellow and brave, but doesn't know how to look after his men, and doesn't try to. I have been fighting with him . . . mainly about the fact that I have no machine, he having given mine to Prince and not managing right about getting me a new one. I think in a few weeks I will be getting pretty sick with the outfit."

In "a few weeks" Kiffin Rockwell was dead, shot down during a patrol. Two days later there was a large funeral held in his honor, and he was posthumously made a Chevalier of the *Légion d'Honneur,* a more coveted decoration than the *Médaille Militaire*.

Three weeks after that Norman Prince was also dead, mortally wounded while escorting Allied bombers during the famous 1916 bombing raid against the German Mauser rifle works at Oberndorf, which shipped twenty thousand rifles a day to the front. He also received the *Légion d'Honneur*. In a classic example of vindictive behavior, the families of both men eventually quarreled about which of them should be interred in the crypt of the beautiful marble Lafayette Escadrille Memorial Monument erected by the French government on the outskirts of Paris after the war. Norman Prince's father attempted to turn the entire monument into a shrine that principally honored his son. When he failed

Fig 18. The members of the Escadrille who attended Norman Prince's funeral in October of 1916. The officer seated third from the left was French Army Captain Georges Thenault, who was the official French commander of the squadron.

in that, he had his son's body removed from the crypt, and eventually had it buried in the National Cathedral in Washington. Kiffin Rockwell remained buried in the cemetery at Luxeuil, near the Escadrille's first airfield, until Prince's body went to Washington, and then Rockwell's family had his body disinterred and buried in the Memorial.

Twenty-two

Colorful Men Arrive on the Eastern Front

In December of 1916 the French aviation high command sent a request to all the French squadrons flying on the Western Front, asking for volunteers to fly in the Army of the Orient. This army consisted of an Allied force that had already been defeated at Gallipoli in an effort to support the Russians on the Eastern Front, but remained capable of maintaining a presence in the part of Greece known as Macedonia. A volunteer from the Lafayette Escadrille named Paul Pavelka ended up flying with this force, and once again Bert Hall played an unusual role, this time involving a different part of the Eastern Front.

Paul Pavelka was the son of a couple who emigrated from Hungary, eventually settling on a farm in Madison, Connecticut. Soon after his mother died at the age of thirty-six as a result of a farm accident involving a pitchfork, his father married Barbara Balogh, described as "a beautiful twenty-two-year-old woman from New York City." Paul, then sixteen, was much nearer this beauty's age than his father was. Infatuated with her, he left home in a state of adolescent turmoil and began a wandering life that included working as a lumberjack in Canada and as a cowboy in Montana. He was in the Panama Canal Zone in 1910, and then went south to participate in a mountain-climbing expedition in the Andes that ended with the deaths of his companions.

When Paul was twenty he spent some years as a sailor, first as a seaman on freighters and then, after joining the United States Navy, on the battleship *Maryland*. Discharged and ending up in Europe in 1914, he joined the Foreign Legion, where his fellow Americans, including Kiffin Rockwell and Alice Weeks's son Kenneth, learned of his seafaring experience and began calling him "Skipper," or "Skip." He was soon caught up in violent fighting. The worst of it came in an attack made in September of 1915 on a German-held woods known as the Bois Sabot in the Champagne region of northeastern France. He and an American named Frank Musgrave were the only two survivors of the forty-man section that entered the fight. Describing the hand-to-hand fighting in another attack, Pavelka said that in lunging back and forth in a bayonet duel with a German, "It was lucky for me he hadn't a longer reach, or he may have done some real damage. As it was he only stuck it in my left leg . . . he won't stick anyone else on this earth with a bayonette or anything else." When Pavelka started flying with the Lafayette Escadrille, Bert Hall said this of him:

"He was with Kiffin Rockwell in the Foreign Legion. Seems, according to Kiffin, that Pavelka saved Kiffin's life when the Legion was attacking up in the north end of the line, somewhere near Arras . . . Kiffin Rockwell had been very desperately wounded, and Pavelka carried him from the field, where he surely would have died, to a dressing station. And all the while, Pavelka was wounded too! So you see, we have a damned good man with us. Needless to say, he and Kiffin are most awfully good friends."

When the call came for pilots to go to the Army of the Orient, Paul Pavelka promptly volunteered. Thus, by the age of twenty-seven, he had become experienced at volunteering. First he had served in the prewar United States Navy. Then he had joined the French Foreign Legion of his free will, and engaged in desperate fighting during which he was wounded. Paul then transferred to the French 170th Infantry Regiment, in which he experienced additional intense combat.

After fighting in the Champagne region, he arrived at Alice Weeks's house, where Paul Rockwell proceeded to take care of him. Then he entered aviation and ended up in the Lafayette Escadrille, joining the unit in August of 1916 in time to engage in dogfights above Verdun. Subsequently based at Cachy in the Somme campaign, he and Adjutant Alfred de Laage of the Escadrille volunteered for missions flown at night to intercept German bombers. In all, Pavelka flew twenty-one of these pioneering missions, including one in which the small electric bulb by which he could see his compass and other panel instruments went out. This forced him to fly for hours in total darkness while being fired at by Allied antiaircraft gunners mistaking him for a lone German raider, until dawn came.

Accepted for service in the Army of the Orient, by February of 1917 he arrived at the Greek port of Salonika, and within four days was at an inland air base from which he immediately began flying a Nieuport two-seater five hours a day over enemy lines. He said this in a letter to a friend:

"I am awfully glad I came to the Orient. It is just what I desired in the line of war. One hundred and eighty kilometres [112 miles] from nowhere, plenty of rough work, and some advancing to keep up the enthusiasm of everyone concerned."

Pavelka thrived in his new surroundings, but many soldiers in the Army of the Orient did not. At the end of July he wrote this:

"It has been very hot here these past few days. So hot that a good many of our boys are being sent to France, as they are not able to stand the [often 120-degree] heat. Malaria reigns supreme. We see many men who are 'dango' from the heat; some become dangerous, and others quite amusing. Leaves are being accorded, and there are about ten thousand *permissionnaires* [men on leave] on their way to sunny France—or rather shady France, for God knows no one would want more sun than there is here in Macedonia."

Fourteen days later, Pavelka was in a nighttime automobile accident in which his driver was crossing a narrow bridge above a boulder-filled ravine without using his headlights. The driver lost control, and the car fell to the rocks below. Pavelka went through the car window, and emerged with cuts on his face, two fractures of the jaw, and two dislocated knees. Within two weeks he resumed flying missions. Pavelka seemed indestructible.

*   *   *

On November 11, he paid a social call on a man whom he
had known in the Legion. This veteran had served at some
point in a cavalry regiment, and that day was supervising
the arrival of some fresh horses, one of which, a mare,
was swiftly convincing an audience of soldiers that she was
"impossible to ride." Pavelka, having spent time as a cowboy
in Montana, asked if he could try to ride this troublesome
mount. With permission granted and a crowd gathering
to watch "the Yankee bronco-buster," a stable-sergeant led
out the mare and held her reins tightly until Pavelka settled
on her back.

Once horse and man were in action, the horse bucked
and reared for a time, with Pavelka successfully hanging on.
Then the frustrated mare changed tactics. She flung herself
to the ground and rolled back and forth on top of Pavelka.
As some men brought her under control and led her away,
others rushed to Pavelka, who lay in the dust with blood
coming out of his mouth.

Paul Pavelka died the next day, and was buried the
following day in a cemetery at Salonika on the coast. The
funeral services were conducted by a British Army chap-
lain, and an English-speaking French clergyman spoke of
the "brave and valuable services" Pavelka had rendered to
France, as well as paying tribute to the friendship between
France and the United States. The American consul and a
guard of honor from a French infantry regiment were present, and one man noted that "all the aviators of the Salonika
sector were there."

*   *   *

Predictably, there would be different versions and inter-
pretations of how, when, and why Bert Hall ended up on
the Eastern Front. All may have been true. It seems that
during the autumn of 1916 a number of the pilots, led
by Norman Prince, apparently began to complain among
themselves about Bert Hall, and decided to run him out
of the squadron. According to this account they saw him
as a roughneck, not fit for the company of gentlemen like
themselves. He was characterized as a liar (often true), as
having forged checks made out to other pilots (probably
true), and as frequently using prostitutes. In particular, they
felt strongly that he had won so much money from them
in their constant card games that he had to be cheating.

Regarding the accusation of cheating, the evidence
favors Bert Hall. He didn't cheat, because he didn't need
to. During the prewar years, when his rich squadron mates
were using their parents' money to play casual poker in their
college clubs and fraternity houses, he had been reading
the poker faces of hardened professional gamblers from all
over Europe. Bert Hall knew the exact odds of whether he
held a better hand than the other man did, and he certainly
knew when a man was bluffing. As for Bert's attitude about
money, he had this to say:

"Aviators in groups on any of the battlefields have an
odd time of it. We play poker, dice, roulette, and if anyone
wins all the money, as someone usually does, it doesn't matter greatly. You go around and borrow what you want and
nobody keeps any account of it, since we know this thing

is going to last a good while and there will be nobody left to worry about debts when it's all over."

When Kiffin Rockwell was killed, his brother Paul, who had great influence with officers of many ranks, was outraged when Bert, instead of attending Kiffin's funeral, allegedly went to Paris to peddle the story of Kiffin's death to the resident American reporters. One study of the Escadrille pilots concluded that this real or imagined slight "was all that Paul Rockwell needed to begin his lifelong smear" of Hall.

As for whether Bert Hall was worthy of being in the company of the other Escadrille pilots, he was on excellent terms with Raoul Lufbery as well as with Bill Thaw. Thaw, who had fought beside him in ground combat with the Legion, said of him, "He was genial, charming, and probably the biggest liar in the Legion . . . always telling us that he had been both a lawman and a bank robber in the western frontier." In a diary entry Hall mentioned the warm hospitality extended to him over a weekend in Paris by Mr. and Mrs. Lawrence Slade, Mrs. Slade being Bill Thaw's sister, who lived in Paris with her husband. Dedicating his book "*En l'Air!*," he paid tribute to "Mr. and Mrs. Lawrence Slade, Who have been Father and Mother to us all—may they live forever." Despite Paul Rockwell's later "lifelong smear" of him, another study of the Escadrille concluded that Paul's brother Kiffin "both admired and respected Hall."

There is photographic evidence as well: In a picture of nine of the pilots including the seven "Founders" taken in the squadron's early days at Luxeuil in May of 1916, Bert Hall and Bill Thaw, the squadron's de facto American leader, are standing beside each other smiling, with their arms linked. No one ever criticized Hall for his behavior when he was fighting side by side with Thaw in the Foreign Legion, and his citations for bravery speak for themselves. His first citation, combining the award of the coveted *Médaille Militaire*—the highest award for valor given to an enlisted man—and also the *Croix de Guerre* with palm, said this:

"After having served in the infantry, been twice wounded, transferred to aviation . . . has very rapidly become a pilot of the first class and very outstanding gunner. Very intelligent, energetic, and most audacious . . . Has fulfilled demanding missions of great peril and danger over German lines on many occasions."

Another citation described him this way: "Clever, energetic, and courageous pilot, full of spirit. Daily attacking enemy planes at very short distance." Nonetheless, the story persists that he was asked to leave the squadron, a story buttressed by a diary entry in which Hall says, "I think the Lafayette Escadrille is glad to get rid of me. I don't blame 'em."

On November 1, 1916, Hall transferred to a nearby French squadron whose commander was a Captain Jean d'Harcourt, whom Bert already knew. Emil Marshall, a nonflying member of the Escadrille, said that as Hall left, he shook his fist at several of the pilots and shouted, "You'll hear from me yet!" He flew successfully with the new squadron for several weeks before he received an extraordinary assignment.

In his "*En l'Air!*" Hall introduced this new experience in a way that leaves open the possibility that he flew in two areas of the Eastern Front: "Early in December, 1916, the French Government received an urgent request from the military in Russia and Romania for some French aviators. They were needed on the east front to show the Russians how we were playing the game, and also to put heart into their fliers."

Next, Hall noted in his diary that "I have orders to report to the under secretary of war in Paris on the morning of December 16th. I don't know what the hell I've done now. Captain d'Harcourt says he thinks it's a special mission and not because of some misdemeanor." Hall reported as ordered, and in his next day's diary entry wrote, "The War Office had me up on the carpet for hours, not giving me hell, but rather telling me what good work I am doing and then telling me how to act in Russia. I am supposed to help the Russians pep up their flying and also report back to Paris what is going on." In a later entry Hall said, "Somehow, I don't believe that the War Office expects me to come back from this blooming mission."

It is at this point that records and chronology mingle and become vague. Bert was told not to keep a diary, and promptly started using a new "dot-and-dash" code in making his diary entries. His earlier statement that he was to "report back to Paris what is going on," in addition to his ominous feeling about "this blooming mission," coincided with a growing feeling among the Allies on the Western Front. They feared that Russia would soon experience a revolution that might take it out of the war and enable the Germans to move many divisions from the Eastern Front to strengthen their position on the Western Front. It might well be that "Paris" was considerably more interested in political than military intelligence. That raised the question of whether Bert Hall was capable of strolling his way through Russia as a spy, a French officer who wore civilian clothes and carried a false French passport as well as his real American one. If unmasked at various checkpoints or during random searches by bands of revolutionary militia, he probably would be shot on the spot.

Once in Russia, for a time he was evidently able to send uncensored mail straight through to Paris. In his diary note of January 26, 1917, from "North-Russian Aviation Base, Litovsk," he wrote, "I hope my messages back to France have some value. Christ knows I am writing everything I can think of. Had letters from the Lafayette today. They are making the war as usual and expect to move soon." He also flew some missions he said would have been considered routine on the "French front" but which brought him high Russian medals and a presentation to the Grand Duke Alexander, who Hall said "asked me questions for two hours."

"We had dinner and it was the first high-class food I have had since I came to this bloody country. The old rule holds good everywhere. If you want to get on in style, hobnob with the upper classes.

"The Grand Duke A. is the only man I have met so far in Russia who seems to understand that four years of major warfare require a social adjustment behind the lines. He said that if Russia came out of the war and withstood the Revolution (which all the nobles seem to expect after the war is over) it would be because the Tsar and his ministers saw fit to bring about some reforms, regulated the

prices of humble necessities and made sure that the under-
classes were not only fed, but treated like human beings.
I thought this was quite a speech, coming from a Russian
Grand Duke."

Bert soon went on to Romania, as part of a 1,600-man
French Army force of advisors and technicians that was struggling to supply and train the badly battered, inept, deficient,
and spiritless Romanian Army. The French were determined
to keep Romania in the war, to protect Russia's southern
flank, but many high-ranking Romanian officers resented
what they considered to be usurpation of their authority.

Out of the 1,600 men of the French Military Mission,
as it was called, only six—Bert and five French pilots—were
assigned to train Romanian pilots. They faced an overwhelm-
ing task. In the course of a month, the nearly useless Romanian Air Force had gone from having forty-four planes and
less than a hundred pilots to receiving 322 aircraft sent from
France, but many of those planes were obsolete and had been
deemed unfit to fly against the Germans. Hall and his French
colleagues set to work, running a small flying school. His
specialty was training the Romanian pilots in target shooting
from a plane. He left few recorded remarks about that, but
found ghastly conditions in war-shattered Romania:

"Thousands of Romanians are dead and tens of thousands are dying from typhus and other epidemics brought
on by famine . . . More than 300,000 people are crowded
into Jassy, a city designed to accommodate about 60,000.
There is little or no food. Doctors and nurses are scarce
and thousands are dying."

He described the suffering in Jassy:

"The cold was intense. There was no wood or coal for heat, and the temperature was about twenty-five degrees above zero. Doctors went through the wards where the wounded lay three to a bed, prodding the men with long goads. If the wounded man grunted he was kept for further treatment; if no grunt was forthcoming, he was buried."

When some of the French pilots went to observe the situation in Russia, Bert went with them. Apparently the morale there had deteriorated since his earlier visit.

"In the Russian aviation things could not have been worse. I found that the men would fly only when they felt like it. They almost never passed over behind the German lines. The average Russian aviator aims to fly six hours per month. His pay is two hundred rubles and after his six hours he takes a good long rest.

"When I started in to really do some flying they thought I was a patriot and a fool. In fact, they didn't make any bones about telling me so. They let the German machines do as they pleased.

"Socially the Russian aviator is a good fellow. They can all play a good game of poker and put away a lot of drinks . . . But as fighters they are nil. No patriotism, no enthusiasm, and not too much courage. About all they did in the aviation corps was drink champagne, play poker and '66,' a German game. They are never in a hurry and don't worry. The Russian has no idea of what war in the air means. They are well equipped, having all of the latest types of fighting machines. But the Russians are not air fighters." He added, apparently of all Russians, "They are not patriotic and care nothing for Russia."

Nonetheless, Bert thought that he might be able to instill some of the "pep" that had been talked about at French Army Headquarters in Paris by finding and fighting a German plane. The opportunity soon came.

"I saw him come over our line at about 1,500 feet altitude and I went after him. I suppose that he thought I was a Russian as he did not pay any attention to me. I proceeded to shoot him down. When I returned I was very much surprised to find that my comrades did not approve of what I had done. They said: 'We have been here a long time and the Germans have never bothered us. Now they will get mad and come and drop bombs on us and may kill some of us.'"

Bert Hall was in Petrograd (St. Petersburg), then the capital of Russia, when the Revolution came. He claimed that the tsar himself awarded him the Cross of St. George, and "only four days later he lost his job." He described the chaos that ensued:

"You can imagine what went on in a city of 3,000,000, during a time like that, with no law and order. All the convicts were liberated, but some of them went back to prison for protection. The people were taking everything they could get their hands on; most of the stores were closed. It was very difficult to get anything to eat and [due to sky-rocketing inflation] rubles were like pennies. Everyone was arrested about twice daily."

Bert decided that it was time to get back to Paris. He first tried to leave via neutral Sweden, but was turned back at Tornio, in Finland. He returned to Petrograd, where various revolutionary factions were killing each other in the streets, and decided to take the Trans-Siberian Railway across Russia to Vladivostok, then go on across the Pacific to the United States before returning to France. According to Hall, before he left he had three meetings with the revolutionary figure Leon Trotsky. At the last of these Trotsky offered him ten thousand dollars and a big diamond ring for his American passport—an offer he said he refused.

Many of Hall's stories are rightly suspect, but his harrowing account of his weeks on a freight train crossing Russia is confirmed by a ship's manifest. From Vladivostok he made his way to Japan, and in Yokohama boarded the *Korea Maru,* to start going on to San Francisco. The passenger list includes Bert Hall, aged forty.

Twenty-three

A Letter from Home, to a Young Man with a Secret

In every unit there is someone who receives a "Dear John" letter. In this case of unrequited love it was new Escadrille member of partially French descent, Edmond Charles Clinton Genet of Ossining, New York, the great-great-grandson of "Citizen" Edmond Charles Genêt, the French Republic's first minister to the United States in 1793. That first Genêt had caused so much trouble with his radical political views on what American foreign policy should be that his government recalled him and strongly intimated that he would be guillotined. The American public was treated to the spectacle of an ambassador begging for asylum from President George Washington, who denounced him for his meddling, but allowed him to stay in the United States. Genêt later married the daughter of New York State's Governor George Clinton, and never returned to France.

That firebrand's descendant, Edmond, was small and sickly, eighteen in 1914, with a baby face, but he enlisted in the Foreign Legion and fought with determined bravery. In addition, he was a charming and ambitious youth who knew how to get things done. Apart from his emotional frustration about the girl back home, Edmond had a secret that could have landed him in trouble on both sides of the Atlantic: He was a deserter from the United States Navy.

Edmond kept an assortment of material that later appeared as a book titled *An American for Lafayette*. The largest portion consists of diary entries combined with letters back to the States, and observations on the war and his part in it. Many of his diary entries have an interesting rhythm to them, a reflection of the "hurry up and wait" reality of war, while others convey an energetic immediacy, a sense of something more than "you are there," but rather, "you are right here beside me, living it with me."

While still in the Foreign Legion in 1915, Edmond wrote a friend back in the States about a day he survived during the Second Battle of Champagne, in the northeast of France: "In an attack we made on Sept. 28th, out of our company of 250 there are not quite 60 left . . . that same night there were but thirty-two of us able to be collected from two companies (500 men) who were able to assist in carrying back behind the lines some of the badly wounded."

Edmond showed a mature sense of the military situation. In February of 1916, fourteen months before the United States entered the war, he wrote this in his diary:

"Fair day. Maneuvers of Moroccan and Colonial Divisions from middle a.m. to late p.m. very interesting but tiring. These maneuvers are certainly very thorough and extensive. The U.S. Army doesn't even dream of such and here the French runs them off even while she is hard at war. Will the U.S. ever be prepared for foreign troubles? It looks doubtful, very doubtful."

In pilot training at the aviation school at Buc, outside of Paris, Edmond demonstrated his philosophical approach to the events of a day:

"Fair day, out practicing on machines in early a.m. Smashed propeller on one machine but learned a valuable lesson from the experience . . . [Later] Practice on machines. Went fairly well in p.m. I certainly have good control when at full speed. Took supper at café in Buc with fellows in evening. Pretty good meal."

In a letter he wrote soon after that, Genet described this: "One American fellow made a Bleriot monoplane look like a match factory scrap heap this morning. He was lucky to come out of it unhurt. The same is liable to occur to any one of us. It's so blamed easy to get kicked out of aviation . . . I don't think much of being sent back to the Legion."

Accidents occurred frequently. In one diary entry, Edmond said this: "Out for work [practice flight] in late p.m. and motor stopped dead while on my second flight. Managed to land without smashing up in a hay field. Mighty thankful for that." The next day he wrote: "Went down to bring back machine I landed with last night. Had to wait four hours while mechanics repaired the motor. Then went up and motor went wrong. Smashed to the ground and broke the machine all to bits and landed in school hospital with a badly wrenched left hip and shoulder. Cleared of negligence [and] all the fellows came over to see me this afternoon."

Two days after that came this: "Fine day. Got out of infirmery [sic] in early a.m. but was told to wait until tomorrow to start flying again . . . Dennis Dowd one of our number was instantly killed last evening in a fall with a Caudron biplane. Was an awful blow to us all. Interment Monday." Dowd had been wounded in trench fighting before being accepted for aviation. While recuperating from that wound, he met a Parisian debutante, Paulette Parent de Saint-Glin; they became engaged and planned to marry after the war.

When Edmond finished pilot training and came to the Escadrille in January of 1917, Pilot Ned Parsons described his dramatic arrival at the frozen, muddy airfield at Cachy in the blood-soaked Somme Valley region of north-central France. On a day when "weather conditions were vile, and the ceiling was so low that even the ducks were walking," all flying had been canceled. The pilots, including Bill Thaw and the attached French lieutenant de Laage, huddled "close to the little pot-bellied stove" and were suddenly "startled by the sound of a plane overhead, down so close to the barracks that the very walls vibrated." The quickly reached consensus was that someone who should never have taken off in this snowstorm was badly lost.

"A few minutes later the door of the mess room burst open and on the wings of a great gust of snow-laden wind a short, muffled, fur-clad figure drifted into the room. Only the tip of a reddish, frostbitten nose and a pair of wide appealing blue eyes showed through the woolen wrappings . . .

"The chunky little figure was topped by a thatch of short-cropped blond hair above the round, innocent pink-cheeked face of an infant. He didn't look a day over fourteen. His peach-bloom complexion showed no traces of ever having met a razor socially. He had a little snubby nose, and there was a constant expression of pleased surprise at the wonders of the world in the wide-set blue eyes. He saluted snappily and in a high-pitched, almost girlish voice announced that he had ferried up a new Nieuport [fighter] from Plessis-Belleville for the Escadrille.

"'Fine work, Corporal,' de Laage congratulated him, 'but it seems to me that you were taking a long chance in this weather.'

"'Oh, I just got so bored, Lieutenant, waiting at Plessis for my orders that when it looked as if the ceiling might lift I just came on.'"

Remembering this, Parsons said, "That was one of Genet's most admirable characteristics, and he had many. He never let difficulties stand in his way. He just plowed through them to the best of his ability. He and Thaw shook hands with the cordiality of old friends, and de Laage suggested, since replacements were so badly needed and since his orders to join the Escadrille were probably in the works, that Genet simply stay instead of going back to Plessis-Belleville. The suggestion was eagerly adopted."

Edmond Genet's friendliness, unfailing courage, and skill in the air soon made him a favorite among his comrades. Despite his youth and relative inexperience as a combat flier, he was often chosen to be the leader of flights into particularly hazardous areas.

The first of young Edmond's problems, though, was his obsession with a clergyman's daughter named Gertrude Talmage, a nineteen-year-old student at Smith College who regarded him as being just a friend. His diary entries contained scores of passages such as this:

"Wrote long letter to adorable Gertrude in evening. What a wonderful loving wife she will make. Oh, God give her to me when I get back to the dear old U.S.A.! Surely ours is a love that will never break!"

Not knowing how to respond to his frequent ardent love letters—a situation complicated by her falling in love with a young Congregational minister from Vermont—Gertrude allowed him to think that his letters had been "lost in the mail." Edmond finally learned the truth from a letter sent by his mother, passing on a letter to her from Gertrude's aunt Mrs. Curry Barlow saying that Gertrude was engaged, and that Mrs. Barlow would also be writing to Edmond. He replied to his mother with these heart-sick words: "The simple truth is unbearable; can you half-imagine what it means to me to have to realize that she has been receiving my letters all these months and has just permitted me to keep on and on without telling me directly and instantly of her engagement?"

In addition to his infatuation with Gertrude, Edmond's other problem was that he had deserted from the United States Navy. Keeping that secret in France would lead him into a unique form of what could be called intelligence work. In 1913, at the age of seventeen, he had enlisted in the United States Navy in a program that he hoped would result in his being accepted at Annapolis and lead to a career as a naval officer. A year later, drawn to the war that was starting to consume Europe, he deserted from the battleship USS *Georgia,* which was in Boston's Charlestown Navy Yard. By February of 1915 he had reached Paris and enlisted in the French Foreign Legion. During his time in the Escadrille, he felt guilty about his desertion, but determined, as he put it, "to throw away my life, if need be, in the war." In letters back to the United States and in visits to Paris, he made efforts to regularize his situation, writing that if he were to be killed—a feeling he never escaped—"it would be much easier if I knew I was O.K. with my own loved country."

In Paris, he became an occasional visitor to Alice Weeks's house, where he became friends with Paul Rockwell. Among the letters in Genet's *An American for Lafayette* there is one to Paul Rockwell in which he thanks Paul for his efforts to help him be accepted for pilot training. In another letter, written on July 21, 1916, he refers to Captain Frank Parker of the United States Army, a West Pointer who was the military attaché at the American Embassy in Paris. At that time the United States was nine months away from entering the war. A military attaché from a neutral country was in a delicate position, in this case not only needing to learn what intelligence he could about the prospective enemy, Germany, but also about France's true military situation and potential. In particular, Parker needed to know more about the French Air Service.

Edmond told Rockwell that he needed "to see the Capt. very badly about a personal matter." In a diary entry he revealed what that "personal matter" was:

"Confess[ed] to the Capt. of my desertion from the Navy. He promised to help me clear myself all he possibly can but advises I hold off action until I've finished my service here. Gave me lots of hope for getting squared later on account of my record here. God grant so."

It became clear that an unspoken bargain had been reached. Edmond Genet, a pilot fully inside the French Army, would provide Captain Parker what information he could about that army's aerial training and tactics. The day after writing about his conversation with Parker, Edmond wrote this in his diary: "Am going to assist Capt. Parker to collect information valuable to the U.S. Service, about aviation, etc." Two weeks later he added this, writing at the flying school at Buc, on the outskirts of Paris:

"Went to Versailles and met Capt. Parker at 11 and brought him out, dined at Hotel Aviatic and showed him the whole school all p.m. Chief Pilot took us around was extremely nice & gave the Capt. a fine impression of me as a pilot."

Nine days later Edmond wrote this, referring to the newly promoted Parker as "Major":

"Worked at Major Parker's office [in Paris] all a.m. Typing a report of the Buc school for him." The next day he recorded that "Major Parker had Lieut. Brekere, Chief Pilot of Buc school in [to Paris] for luncheon." The day after that, "Went to see Colonel Girod, Comdt. of Aviation with Major Parker in early a.m. and rec'd permission to go to [advanced training] school at Pau instead of Avord." In another entry he defined his mission once more: "Getting all information possible about machines used in the war for future use. May be of help to U.S. Aviation Corps."

For a youth who had recently turned nineteen—he was the youngest pilot in the Escadrille—Edmond demonstrated quite a talent for bringing influential people to his side. Among those who helped him realize his ambition to become a pilot was Dr. Gros, the Escadrille's principal organizer and fund-raiser, who "said he knew of me and would do all possible for me." Jarousse de Sillac, the diplomat who held a prominent post in the Ministry of Foreign Affairs, assured him of his support: Edmond said of two letters he received from de Sillac, "He may help me greatly to get into aviation."

When he was accepted for pilot training, Edmond scarcely lacked for social acquaintances. "Miss Ann Morgan, daughter of J. Pierpont Morgan [Jr.] . . . motored out from their home in Versailles to see us all and asked Capt. to allow us all to come to lunch with them someday, possibly Saturday. They can give us a fine time so hope we can go."

Serious as he was about flying, Edmond had other sides to his life. In early training at Buc, he wrote, using colloquial language of the day, "Started practice with our new baseball team in a.m. Created quite a sensation among the blamed Frenchmen." In addition to baseball, Genet played soccer, describing it by its European name. "Played football a little bit in early a.m. Don't care for the Association game the French always play. It's slow and unscientific."

Brief references show the camaraderie: "Out at café with the Bunch all evening and had fine time singing and forgetting old cares." Another reference to off-duty evenings contained this: "Had supper in village east of school [Buc] with fellows & all went to Hotel Aviatic afterwards where we played the piano and had some drinks and champagne. Not enough to harm anyone." In addition to that, Edmond carried on a prolific correspondence with twenty or more relatives and friends in the United States, several of whom sent him packages containing clothes, nonperishable food, and books. He also became a favorite of many Americans of different ages living in Paris.

In the Escadrille, dogfights came quickly. On February 15, 1917, Edmond made this diary entry:

"Superb day. Out along our lines from 8:30 to 10:30 this morning with [Ronald] Hoskier and Parsons and we all had several hot, close combats with two German planes over Roye. Had a fight with each of them in turn being attacked by one as I was driving the other down to earth. Had to leave off chasing the first to turn and attack the second which I forced to quit and dive for safety at 400 metres over Roye and several batteries of anti-aircraft guns which quickly opened up a furious fire at me. I think I killed the gunner of the second . . . Aerial combats certainly are exciting and soon over. They try one's nerves to the limit but there is very little if any time to think of danger to one's self."

Edmond's eloquence and compassion came to the fore when he learned that Kiffin Rockwell, flying in a different area, had been killed while attacking a two-seater German Albatros. He wrote this letter to Kiffin's brother Paul, who was at Alice Weeks's house in Paris.

"My dear Paul,

"My heart took a mighty big drop for you this afternoon when I read in the paper of Kiffin's death at the front and my very deepest sympathy goes out to you in this untimely loss. If you can console yourself at all console yourself in the fact that your brother's end came while he was hero-ically defending this big cause, for which we all are willing to give our lives, in the face of the enemy. I earnestly hope that as glorious a fate awaits us as Kiffin found . . .

"My sympathy goes out, too, to Mrs. Weeks for I know this sad loss only intensifies her own past sorrow. Please extend to her my deepest regards.

"Try to brighten up, dear Paul. Your brother has found a glorious end—a soldier's death and, 'tho it has come far too soon and unexpected, such a death should tend to soften the hardness of the personal loss and bereavement. May you find it so.

"Always faithfully yours—
Edmond C. C. Genet"

Six weeks after writing his condolence letter to Paul Rockwell, Edmond made this diary entry:

"This is my 20th birthday. Wish it was my 18th. The years are flying too fast. Much too fast." Despite his youthful energy, Edmund occasionally wrote about having stomach trouble, and noted that flying thousands of feet up in an open cockpit resulted on one occasion in his returning from a mission "with ice all around my nose and mouth." During that harsh winter of 1917, one evening he made the diary entry, "Fine day but so cold that I have had to melt the ink in my fountain pen in order to write this."

Edmond found himself directly involved in the next Escadrille death. James McConnell, whose book *Flying for France* had just been published to favorable reviews in the United States, had experienced a return of severe rheumatism caused by an earlier back injury suffered in a crash landing. Captain Thenault had ordered him back to the hospital for further treatment, but after some days there McConnell left, against doctor's orders, and returned to the Escadrille.

On Monday, March 19, 1917, Edmond took off on a three-plane patrol to protect French observation planes that were scouting above the little town of Ham in the Somme Valley. The Escadrille pilots were Ned Parsons, Edmond, and McConnell, who was not supposed to be back on duty. Parsons experienced motor trouble soon after takeoff, and had to return to base. Edmond described what happened then.

"'Mac' and I kept on—he leading . . . North of Ham I discovered two German machines much higher than we coming towards us to attack. One was much nearer than

Lowell.   Genet.   Lufbery.   Mac Connell

Fig 19. The man on the right in this picture, using a device that kept a map under control in an open cockpit, is pilot James McConnell, a 1910 graduate of the University of Virginia, from where he was nearly expelled for placing a chamber pot on the head of a statue of Thomas Jefferson. Three hours after this photograph was taken, McConnell was killed in action. He had left a note to be read if he died. It said in part: "My burial is of no import. Make it as easy as possible for yourselves . . . Good luck to the rest of you. God damn Germany and *vive la France*."

the other and began to come towards 'Mac.' I immediately started up towards it and met it at 2200 metres—leaving Mac to take care of the [lower] end.

"The German Avion [aircraft] was a biplane and his gunner opened up on me at 200 yards as the pilot began to circle around me. I opened fire with my incendiary [tracer] bullets and headed directly for them. The German's first few shots cut one main wing support in half and an explosive bullet hit the guiding rod of the left aileron [wing control flap] and cut open a nice hole in my left cheek. I scarcely noticed it and kept on firing until we were scarcely 25 yds apart. We passed close and . . . [I dove] down. The German didn't follow but an anti-aircraft battery shelled me for quite awhile. At 1000 metres I stopped and circled around for 15 minutes in search of Mac and the second Boche but the clouds were thick and I saw nothing.

"I was afraid my supports would break entirely and my wound was hurting some so I headed for St. Just at a low altitude reaching there at 10:45 hoping all the way back that Mac had preceded me but when I arrived I found he had not and tho Lufbery and Lt. de Laage have been out over the region north of Ham with their SPAD to look for him (de Laage landed to ask the troops if they saw him brought down) they found nothing and the chances are Mac was either brought down by the German machine or else wounded in combat and brought down in their territory and so is a prisoner. It's the best we can hope for—that he is at least alive.

"I feel dreadfully—my wound, tho painful, is nothing compared with my grief for poor 'Mac's loss. The Commandant told me, when I described the combat to him this morning, that I fought bravely. I wish I had been able to do more for McConnell."

Thenault, accompanied by Lieutenant de Laage and two or three American pilots, drove out to where McConnell had crashed. They found his body, punctured by several bullets, lying near the wreckage of his plane in an apple orchard on the edge of a village named Detroit Bleu. The Germans had stripped off his flying outfit, also taking his boots, "dog tags"—worn for identification—and watch.

A peasant woman approached and told them that she had seen the plane dueling with one German, and then another had dived in from behind and shot it down.

After the men of the Escadrille pulled together what they finally knew about their comrade's death and his wishes, they buried him in the earth where he died. In a letter he had written to be read in the event of his death, he left his sleeping bag to Ned Parsons, and added:

"My burial is of no import. Make it as easy as possible for yourselves. I have no religion and do not care for any service. If the omission would embarrass you, I presume I could stand the performance. Good luck to the rest of you. God damn Germany and *vive la France*."

When a memorial service for McConnell was held at the American Church in Paris on April 2, 1917, according to one account, "Three tearful mesdemoiselles attended, each one believing she was McConnell's fiancée. One would later marry another Lafayette Escadrille pilot."

Two days after that, Genet wrote this diary entry:

"975th day of the conflict. [Escadrille pilot Robert] Soubiran arrived from Paris with the great news that the United States has declared war against Germany and Paris is decorated with Old Glory everywhere . . .

"Somehow I've given way completely this evening. I feel sure there is something very serious going to happen to me very soon. It doesn't seem any less than Death itself. I've never had such a feeling or been so saddened since coming over to battle for this glorious France. I tore into shreds a little silken American flag which I've carried since the beginning of my enlistment. Sometimes it seems a mockery to rejoice over the entrance of our country into the conflict with the Entente when we have been over here so long giving our all for the right while our country has been holding back. She should have been in long ago."

He also expressed bitterness about two unnamed pilots who he felt shirked their duty:

"Neither of them seem to be very enthusiastic fighters and take every possible opportunity to remain at the camp on pretense of being sick or tired and the rest of us break our necks and even lose our lives to keep up the good service of the Escadrille.

"Those two I'm convinced will see the finish of the war, return to America, and pose as the heros [sic] of the Escadrille and be accepted as such by those who don't know any better."

On Sunday, April 15, Edmond made this entry in his flight logbook: "Felt almost nauseated in the air this time. Stomach was in poor shape." The next day he felt worse. "Saw a Boche Biplane . . . He dove below the clouds when I swung around to dive on him . . . We were shelled [by antiaircraft fire] at that moment . . . One shell, the first, came very close to my tail. The motion of continually turning in all directions and levels made me feel very sick so I had to return to camp. Stomach was very upset."

The next morning, when Edmond and a pilot named Walter Lovell returned from a patrol during which they saw nothing, Lovell commented on his "sunken features and waxlike complexion." Genet went to bed, but asked to be wakened for the afternoon patrol. Another pilot, Willis Haviland, offered to fly in Edmond's place, but he shook his head.

At 2:30 that afternoon, Edmond took off, following Lufbery. As they came to enemy lines, Lufbery looked back and saw three shells burst a hundred yards behind Genet. Edmond turned his plane around and headed back to their base. Lufbery also turned around and followed Edmond for what he noted as being four minutes. Seeing that Edmond was flying straight and level, Luf turned again and completed the patrol.

French soldiers at the front reported what happened next. Less than three minutes after Edmond's plane crossed back over friendly lines at four thousand feet, flying at full speed, it went into a violent spin. A wing fell off and the plane dropped like a rock, smashing into the ground three hundred yards from where his friend Jim McConnell had been killed.

No one ever knew whether Edmond had been too sick to control his plane, or whether the antiaircraft fire had wounded him in some way that rendered him unconscious. Willis Haviland, who had offered to fly in his place, drove out to the crash site "to get his body," accompanied by Ned Parsons. Parsons said of Edmond's remains, "Every bone in his body was broken and his features were completely gone."

Edmond Genet, aged twenty, was buried in a little cemetery at the air base at Ham, eighty miles north of Paris. A light snow fell as the coffin was lowered into the grave. He had left an earlier undated note that said, "If I die, wrap me in the French flag, but place the two colors upon my

grave to show that I died for two countries." In accordance
with his instructions, his body was wrapped in the French
flag and placed in the coffin. Then an American flag and a
French flag were wrapped around the coffin, and a slender
plain wooden cross placed on top of it.

Invoking the biblical Benjamin, Captain Thenault said
this as he stood in the snow beside Edmond's coffin:

"He was young, and he seemed even younger. He was
our Benjamin, and we cherished him as in a family one
prefers the youngest, the weakest. But his heart was not
weak, as on many occasions he caused us to see."

As Thenault finished his tribute, a shaft of sunlight cut
through the falling snow.

When Edmond died, his mother wrote to Josephus Daniels, the United States secretary of the Navy, giving him all
the facts, including that Edmond had been posthumously
awarded the *Croix de Guerre* with two palms. Daniels had
the record of desertion expunged and wrote her this:

"Edmond Charles Genet, having honorably termi-
nated an enlistment with an ally, since he died on the field
of battle . . . I am myself honored in having the privilege
of deciding that the record of Edmond Genet, ordinary
seaman, United States Navy, shall be considered in every
respect an honorable one."

Twenty-four

The United States Enters the War

While Bert Hall was on his secret trip, combat units of the United States Army began arriving at French ports in late June. On the Fourth of July, 1917, they were to march through Paris in their first appearance before the French public. Another Escadrille pilot named Hall, James Norman Hall, destined for future fame as the co-author of *Mutiny on the Bounty,* stood quietly on a sidewalk, wearing his French uniform, and wrote this in a letter home:

"At 8 a.m. about two thousand of the American Troops began their parade. I awaited them at the Place de la Concorde. What a sight! I felt like crying. Marching to music they went on up the Rue de Rivoli to the Hotel de Ville [City Hall]. The streets were packed with people. The ranks were broken up by the crowds. I never saw such a demonstration. Everywhere were American flags. Everybody was yelling, jumping, shouting, all through the three hours' parade. French poilus burst into the lines and took our boys by the arms, marching and singing with them. Women did the same, and all the women were weeping.

"Then they came to the Hotel de Ville and the "Star-Spangled Banner" was played. Every Frenchman, Englishman, Belgian, and American bared his head and silently stood at attention. The music stopped and for a few moments there was silence; then the crowds burst again into a tremendous cheer, and the parade went on to the tomb of Lafayette. Paris was wild, frantic. I never saw anything like it. They are crazy over the Americans. "*Vive l'Amerique!*" seems still to be buzzing in my ears. I can't begin to describe the wonderful effect our declaration of war has on the French. It has given them new courage. We came in at the psychological moment. France weeps for happiness; cheers for joy; rekindles her spirit and cries, "*Vive l'Amerique!*"

"I left the parade at the Hotel de Ville. I was too weak, trembling, and too full of emotion to go any farther. My last impression was the picture of General Pershing [John J. Pershing, commander of the American Expeditionary Force], riding through the frantic mob, with his hand at a constant salute. I don't think he took his hand down once through the whole three hours' procession except when he spoke and the flag was dedicated."

The United States entered the war at a time when the exhausted French Army was experiencing mass desertions. In contrast, the morale and efficiency of the Escadrille was steadily improving. As the American Expeditionary Force

Fig 20. This picture of Escadrille pilot James Norman Hall, who would gain future fame as coauthor of *Mutiny on the Bounty*, was taken by one of his German captors shortly after he was shot down behind enemy lines. Hall, who at the time sported a large handlebar moustache, is pictured above in a German staff car, waiting for the next steps in his captivity. His broken nose has been bandaged, and both his ankles were severely sprained in the crash. The calm-looking dachshund in his lap presumably belongs to one of the Germans. Hall finished the war behind bars at Landshut Castle in Bavaria.

began arriving in France in mid-1917, the United States Army Air Service had little strength to contribute. The Air Service existed largely on paper: In the entire United States it had only two operational flying fields, and fifty-five planes. General Pershing said of those aircraft, ". . . 51 were obsolete, and the other four were obsolescent."

The senior American Air Service officers wanted to take over all the American pilots flying for France. The plan was to keep them low in rank so that, with few exceptions, they would be outranked by most of the Air Service pilots, none of whom had ever flown in combat. As for being sticklers for regulations, the newly arrived American commanders started off by requiring that these veteran airmen start wearing cavalry spurs on their military boots—something guaranteed to tear apart the delicate interior of a fighter plane's cockpit. Additionally, they wanted all these pilots who had served with the French to take the rigorous American pilot physical exam.

All of this produced a lot of resistance, and Ned Parsons, now an ace, wrote a withering critique in which he stated that many of the pilots who had excelled in combat during the first three years of the war could not possibly pass that test.

In any event, some of the American pilots stayed with the French, but most were soon flying in American squadrons that used French planes. The performance and past records of those who had flown with the French began to convince the senior officers of the United States Army Air Service that they deserved promotions. Bill Thaw ended the war as a squadron commander with the rank of major, having received American decorations that included the Distinguished Service Cross, the nation's second-highest medal for valor.

In line with Ned Parsons' comment that many of the successful Escadrille pilots could not pass the American physical, the authorities began to grant medical waivers. The most interesting of these was given to Dudley Hill, who could see out of only one eye. Dated November 17, 1917, and signed by General Pershing, it read in part, "On account of three years flying with the French army it is thought he would make a very useful officer in spite of marked vision defect." Hill justified the decision, going on to be a captain and the commander of an American Army fighter squadron.

All of the Allied commanders were slow to grasp the difference between tactics—how a squadron handled an enemy met on its patrols and the result of those meetings—and the bigger strategic picture. Gradually they began to realize that while sound tactics that produced kills and saved Allied planes were important, it was of equal importance to record where the kills took place and where groups of enemy and Allied planes were assigned.

Just by putting a superior number of fighter planes into a given area, the Allies reduced the enemy's chances of conducting successful reconnaissance or bombing missions there, and possibly forced enemy commanders to move more of their squadrons into areas to which they had wanted to assign a lower priority.

On the other hand, by assigning too few planes to a particular area, the Allies risked losing an inordinate number of their own planes. For example, in initially assigning American squadrons their areas of operation the French failed to put into practice what they had learned about the importance of keeping sufficient numbers of planes in strongly contested sectors. The pilots in some of the American squadrons proved themselves to be well trained and skillful, but during what turned out to be the German buildup to their offensive at Château-Thierry, fifty miles east-northeast of Paris, the French assigned only one flight of six to ten American planes to patrol a ten-mile stretch of the front. They assigned only one more American flight of six to ten men to each of two more ten-mile spans, one on each side of the central area. This left, at most, only thirty American planes to patrol a hotly contested thirty-mile front.

That resulted in the most desperate fighting the United States Army fliers engaged in during their time at the front. As many as twenty-four German fighters would pounce on a single formation of as few as six American planes, with predictably merciless results. When this enormous disparity was corrected, the reinforced American squadrons went on to play a successful part in one of the hardest-fought and most important victories of the war—that at Château-Thierry.

Twenty-five

A Lion in the Air Passes the Torch, and the Escadrille Bids Its Own Lions Farewell

After bringing Ernst Udet out of the mud in Flanders by inviting him to join his "Flying Circus," the "Red Baron" Manfred von Richthofen soon gave him command of Jasta 11, the legendary German squadron he had led himself before becoming a group commander. Udet wrote of Richthofen vividly and insightfully, describing his strong Teutonic features and arresting blue eyes. Being privy to Richthofen's combination of aerial tactics and strategic thinking, he observed that Richthofen initiated the practice of establishing a forward base, placing his squadrons so near the front lines that his pilots could fly five missions a day, compared with the three missions averaged by the British and French units that had to fly farther just to reach the area where dogfights occurred. Udet said of his leader, "He was the least complicated man I ever knew. Entirely Prussian and the greatest of soldiers."

Uncomplicated or not, Richthofen had developed a tactic that Allied airmen never fully understood. He would open fire from behind an enemy plane at a distance of several hundred yards. The chances of doing significant damage from that range were slim, but when the pilot realized that a hostile plane was firing at him from behind he would begin zigzagging, to present a more difficult target. Every second he spent swerving from side to side was a second that Richthofen used to fly straight ahead, shortening the distance until he was close enough to execute one of his scores of kills.

Again, for a simple man, Richthofen had a penetrating view of the mind-set of the fliers of different nationalities. Writing in his diary in February of 1917, he said of his and his group's quest for victories, "Everything depends on whether we have for opponents those French tricksters or those daring rascals, the English. I prefer the English. Frequently their daring can only be described as stupidity. In their eyes it may be pluck and daring."

Richthofen offered up his own German ethnic characterization:

"In my opinion the aggressive spirit is everything and that spirit is very strong in us Germans. Hence we shall always retain the domination of the air.

"The French have a different character. They like to put traps and to attack their opponents unaware. That cannot easily be done in the air. Only a beginner can be caught and one cannot set traps because an airplane cannot hide itself. The invisible airplane has not yet been discovered.

Sometimes, however, the Gallic blood asserts itself. The Frenchmen will then attack. But the French attacking spirit is like bottled lemonade. It lacks tenacity.

"The Englishmen, on the other hand, one notices that they are of Germanic blood. Sportsmen take easily to flying, and Englishmen see in flying nothing but a sport. They take a perfect delight in looping the loop, flying on their back, and indulging in other sports for the benefit of our soldiers in the trenches. All these tricks may impress people who attend a Sports Meeting, but the public at the battle-front is not as appreciative of these things. It demands higher qualifications than trick flying. Therefore, the blood of English pilots will have to flow in streams."

As for his overall philosophy of victory in the air, Richthofen repeated his belief in taking the offensive: "The aggressive spirit, the offensive, is the chief thing everywhere in war, and the air is no exception." He combined his iron determination with a chivalric fatalism, saying, "Fight on and fly on to the last drop of blood and fuel—to the last beat of the heart and the last kick of the motor: a death for a knight—a toast for his fellows, friend and foe."

When Richthofen was fatally shot down on April 21, 1918, Udet, already the victor in forty-two dogfights, was on leave at home in Munich, nursing an ear infection and becoming reacquainted with his childhood sweetheart, Eleanor Zink, known as "Lo," whom he later married. Despite his doctor's advice that his ear had not healed and he should postpone any flying, he returned to the front and was one of the pilots saved by the recent introduction of the parachute. On June 29, 1918, he jumped as his plane was going down after being disabled by gunfire from a French fighter. Udet's luck was with him again: His parachute harness became entangled with his plane's rudder, and he reached up and broke off the tip of the rudder just in time for the parachute to open, 250 feet above the ground. He survived with a broken ankle.

That August Ernst Udet reached his zenith, bringing down *twenty* more enemy planes, most of them British. In a dogfight on September 28, 1918, a bullet wounded him in the thigh. He was still recovering when the war ended six weeks later. Udet had outlived the other great ones: With sixty-two victories, second only to Richthofen's eighty, he was alive, whereas Max Immelmann, the pilot who devised the tactic known as "The Immelmann Turn"; Otto Boelcke, whom Richthofen considered to be his mentor and tutor; and Richthofen himself, were dead. While Udet was gone, another noted fighter pilot ace named, Hermann Goering, a man who shot down twenty-two Allied planes, had taken command of the "Flying Circus."

Twenty-one years later, Colonel General Ernst Udet was second-in-command of the Luftwaffe, the German Air Force, led by Reichsmarschall Hermann Goering, in a Germany controlled by Adolf Hitler, who in 1918 was an obscure penniless Austrian serving as a lance-corporal in the Bavarian Army.

Despondent over Goering's lies to Hitler about Germany's aircraft production and then his blaming of material shortages on Udet, as well as what he saw as Hitler's fatal decision to attack the Soviet Union, Udet committed suicide by shooting himself in the head on November 17,

Fig 21. Captain Hermann Goering, the famous fighter pilot and future number two Nazi who took command of von Richthofen's unit when the leading ace was killed. At his throat he has the Pour le Mérite, Germany's highest medal for valor, also won by von Richthofen and Boelcke.

1941. The Nazi authorities released the news of his death in stories saying that he had died while testing a new weapon. Ernst Udet was buried next to Manfred von Richthofen in a Berlin cemetery.

The Lafayette Escadrille was officially dissolved on February 18, 1918. Some of its members who had joined the

American Air Service in 1917 wanted to keep their lion mascots Whiskey and Soda, but were informed that they were to be sent to the Paris Zoo. Edward Hinkle, the oldest of the Escadrille pilots, who had developed bronchial problems and was on nonflying status, remembered the parting:

"Luf and Whiskey were great pals, so Luf volunteered to take Whiskey to the Paris Zoo. I went along. It was a great lark for Whiskey, who loved to ride. He sat between us in the front of the truck. It was a sad thing to see the cage door close on him. We visited Whiskey whenever we had Paris leave, and he always recognized us. [Another account said that Soda lived in the same cage, and that the lions would roll over on their backs to have their stomachs scratched.] Both Whiskey and Soda died soon after the war of rheumatism, or maybe loneliness."

Twenty-six

Yvonne!

The most confusing and contradictory part of Bert Hall's wartime story involves his movements in 1917 and 1918. In addition to everything else he did, this was apparently the time during which he wrote "*En l'Air!*" In light of the circumstances under which he left the Escadrille, he displayed a remarkably generous attitude toward his former squadron mates. In a chapter titled "My Pals," he praised thirteen of them by name, and closed the chapter with, "Wouldn't any American be proud to have lived and fought with a bunch like this!"

According to Hall, after he'd traveled from Moscow to Vladivostok on the Trans-Siberian Railway, he crossed the Pacific on a freighter, spent several months in the United States, and arrived back in France at the port of Le Havre on January 19, 1918. Other records indicate that he was still in the United States at that time and later, but his diary has a certain Bert Hall-ish quality that seems authentic. Reaching

Paris two days later, he wrote this: "Of all people, who should I see today but Lufbery. He was standing at the desk in the Grand Hotel. Of course, we talked, and talked. He said I had been reported as dead." They had time to do a few days of intensive partying before Luf went back to his flying in the new American squadron to which he now belonged.

Lufbery not only continued to knock down German planes, but led the American Air Service pilots who were new to the front on their first combat patrols. Among them was Lieutenant Eddie Rickenbacker, on his way to being the foremost American Expeditionary Force ace. He would later say, "Everything I learned, I learned from Lufbery."

When Hall got back to the Western Front himself after being debriefed at French Army headquarters in Paris, he was reassigned to Escadrille SPAD-3, the best of the five best French squadrons, all of whose members were known as the "*Cigognes*," or "Storks." He wanted to get back to serious fighting in the air, and was allowed to do a few days of that, but both the French and American authorities now saw him as doing something more useful than acting as additional aerial cannon fodder.

The French summoned him back to headquarters. Because he was a man who still had to take orders, no matter what he thought of them, he went. Dispiritedly, he wrote this in his diary:

"They have placed me at the disposal of the Intelligence Section of the French Air Service, and I am to do counter-espionage. I asked one of the lieutenants at Headquarters if he had any idea how this had come about. I had known him long ago, back in 1915 in the Champagne country.

"He said, 'Yes, that's easy. Your record as a pilot is very good—excellent, in fact. You did fairly well in Russia, to spy on them for six months and come away with all their decorations—alive in the bargain. You speak several languages, and then as a liar you're quite versatile. So, with that, they decided to make you a counter-espion [counterspy]. Voila!'

"After that, the Lieutenant and I went and had lunch."

The French wanted Bert Hall for counterespionage, but the Americans had a different plan for him. After he engaged in some more intense aerial combat in a French squadron, the Americans asked him to report to the American Air Service headquarters in Paris. He wrote in his diary, "They told me that I was to do a motion picture and take it to America for the purpose of encouraging recruiting in the Air Section." During yet another session, he was told that he was to go back to the United States and sell the Liberty Bonds then being sold in support of the war.

Hall had sensed that both the French and the Americans saw him as their property, but that the Americans did not intend to make him the subject of a bureaucratic wrangle. That proved to be the case. Thus he was able to divide his time between combat flying near Amiens in northern France and working as a counterespionage agent for the French. He had a lot of flexibility in his schedule; after four years of war and his intelligence work, he knew a lot about how the war was progressing. His ability to move around behind the Western Front led him into an interesting relationship, which he began to record in his diary.

"By previous arrangement, I went over to a little hut not far from the village of Lamotte and had dinner tonight with some English aviators. The place is run by a snotty-nosed old woman with a limp and a bleary eye, and a very beautiful young waitress. The waitress is, of course, named Yvonne. She would be named Yvonne. And, she's good lookin'! She's as pretty as the old female is ugly.

"I ordered the dinner in French, of course, and while we were waiting, the Limey got to lapping up a little red ink. One of the lads got rather oiled up and called the old girl in to tell her exactly how he wanted his rations. He talked in English, throwin' in a little bad French now and then. Finally the old wench nodded her head and went away. The pilot I know best in the outfit (his name is Binner) said:

" 'Edgar, all your chaff was lost on the old 'un. She knows as little about the King's English as a sow does about spicin' a puddin'!'

" 'Is that so!' said a voice behind us, and there stood the old wench with a handful of knives and forks—dribbly nose and all! 'Is that so!' and her English accent was quite upper class. 'Well, young man, if your luck is as sharp as your tongue, you might live long enough to find out you're mistaken!' And she went on cooking our dinner.

"I discovered later that Yvonne was the old woman's niece. And all of us discovered that Yvonne speaks English—not awfully well, but well enough. I shall go back to that place. That Yvonne person is a whiz-bang. She has a complexion like an unplucked peach and her teeth are clean too.

"The dinner was considered to be a great success. I don't know whether I like this spy gag or not, but I suppose I'll have to like it—they'll make me like it."

The next day Bert Hall flew the dawn patrol, and later recorded what he did after that.

"Lieutenant Binner, several other Limey pilots, an Aussie flier named McCormick, and I went over to Yvonne's place tonight. Yvonne was more radiant than ever. The other lads are keeping hands off in favor of me. Just why, I don't know, but I suppose they are just giving a gauche American a chance to queer himself before they start making their hypnotic passes. This may be unkind, but who can tell.

"Yvonne's last name is Dacree; she was born in France of a French father and an English mother. Both parents have been bumped off since the beginning of the war. The old bleary-eyed aunt is named Patterson, and she was originally English. They have an estate and rather a fine one up near Cambrai. It's inside the English lines, but the war is a bit too hot for the women folks just now, so the Government sent them back as far as Amiens.

"On the way, the old girl started up this little restaurant. If the war lasts long enough the Patterson-Dacree family will recoup their losses because the little restaurant is damned successful . . . How old lady Patterson gets the raw materials for the things she puts out is the one unsolved mystery of the war."

As so often happened, the weather brought flying operations to a halt. Hall began a diary entry with: "Dud weather— no ceiling at all—fog right down on the ground." For Bert Hall, being the man he was, the fog presented an opportunity.

"I went over to visit with Binner and together we went to old lady Patterson's for lunch. I told Yvonne that I was going to Paris and asked her what she wanted me to bring back in the way of a little gift. She said she wanted a special kind of comb for her hair and a pair of colored silk stockings. I told her I'd bring two pairs if she would give me the top of one stocking after she had worn it, so I could wear it under my helmet for luck.

"Binner is a smart bastard. All the while this conversation was going on, he appeared not to listen and then afterwards, he said:

"'Christ, laddie, how you Americans do clear the hurdles with a woman! You cover the first ninety-nine obstacles in one leap. How do you do it, now really!'

"I said, 'Oh, that's nothing; it's just what you fellows call "getting on with the jolly old war."'

"He said, 'Of course, you mean to do right by the little peach!'

"And I said, 'Listen, brother, I mean to do quite as right by the little peach as the little peach means to do right by me and if you've lived in France any time at all, particularly during the war, you know what I'm getting at.'

"Binner seemed to know. He simply said, and very English-like, 'Oh, yes, yes, old man, of course, of course.'

". . . Nevertheless, Yvonne is a darling and I'm going to bring her the silk socks, if I go broke doing it, and the hair ornament too." After a leave in Paris combined with bringing back a new SPAD to fly at the front, Hall wrote this:

"Had dinner at Yvonne's. She was radiant about her 'coming back' gift. Ate alone though. Binner is finished off.

They got him the afternoon of the 15th . . . Both Yvonne and old lady Patterson shed tears as they told me of it.

"I finally convinced Yvonne that she must wear one pair of the stockings before she cut off the top as a return souvenir to me. She said:

"'Very well, if I must. I shall wear them and wash them all nice and clean and then you can make a stocking cap out of the top.'

"Of course, she was all wrong. There would be no washing. It was a rather delicate matter to explain. I wanted her to give me something she had worn next to her skin, so that I could wear it next to my skin—and without washing too. When she finally understood, she blushed the most beautiful blush I have ever seen and that was all. She knew and I knew, and that's all that mattered.

"As I left, she went to the door with me. At the door, I caught her arm and together we went outside into the darkness. She knew what would happen. And it did! There were only two sentences spoken. She said I must fly carefully and I told her good night. But there was a space of time when nothing was said."

Two days later, Hall wrote about impending German offensives and the need to bring more planes from Paris because "we are not going to be caught without equipment." Then this:

"I have the top of Yvonne's stocking. The bottom can still be used, she tells me. It seems that I got a very long length. The top was all crumpled up and smelled faintly of some kind of perfume. I asked her why it was crumpled up and she said I was being too naïve. She said how did I suppose a girl kept her stockings from falling down, and then I understood. The top had been wrapped around her garter; she called it 'the elastic.'

After all, there *is* no fool like an old fool. Here I am a hardened old woman chaser, eating out of a twenty-year-old girl's hand, and liking it too, and loving it too. If I could only invent some way of getting Yvonne away from the old gorgon for a little while! Yvonne is more than willing, but the old girl has eyes like two hawks. Tonight, as we were standing outside in the dark, Yvonne told me that her lips were curiously hungry for me. It's been a long time since I've listened to talk like that. These school girls are surely alive when it comes to making love. An old man never realizes how antique his technique is until he encounters one of these youngsters."

In a sense, the war kept playing a capricious role in Bert Hall's love life. Here he was, gambling for the highest stakes—his life—in a supremely perilous occupation, while Yvonne saw it as an interesting flirtation with an older man. Three days after noting that Yvonne said that "her lips were curiously hungry for me," he flew a mission in which he said he "ran into an archy [antiaircraft] burst and just made a landing field by the skin of my teeth. Was wearing Yvonne's stocking top too. It must have been the stocking off the wrong leg. Plane shot full of holes—will have to have a new one."

As if near-fatal German antiaircraft shells were not enough of a problem, the next day Hall encountered this:

"At Headquarters, they tell me that I'm not a very good counter-espion, because they say I'm too obvious. I told 'em I didn't ask for the job and that they could climb a tree with the Intelligence Service and stay there with it, but they decided not to go to that much trouble. I'll possibly [be ordered to] go back to the trenches."

Soon the veteran gambler thought his hand of cards might be filling in better than he had thought it would. He was told to go to Paris and pick up a new plane, and thought he could include Yvonne in the short leave he was given to do that.

"At last I have Yvonne into the notion of going to Paris for a brief holiday. She has convinced the old gorgon that it's the thing to do. I, of course, am not in the picture at all. Yvonne has some very near relatives (on her father's side) in Paris and the old gorgon seems to think that Yvonne might visit them to the advantage of all concerned. I see the little dear secretly—at least I hope it's secretly. One can never tell, with such a sharp-eyed bird as Madame Patterson snooping around all the time.

"I'm supposed to go up to Paris on the 27th and if my luck holds out, Yvonne will be on the same train. I am not planning beyond the train. We could stop off at Clermont, but I suppose it's best to let events take care of themselves.

"Since my tough luck of the 23rd [with antiaircraft shells], I'm not so sold on Yvonne's stocking top. It would appear that I had better luck before I took on that bauble, but then war is not all good luck."

The following day, this:

"Short hop this a.m. and later a visit to Yvonne's place. She thinks it's better for me to come over and eat dinner now and then to keep the old girl from getting suspicious. I don't mind. Tomorrow we take off for Paris. I am to meet the girl on the train. Somehow, I don't believe it will happen, but tomorrow will tell. Incidentally, I do *not* go to the trenches."

The next day, a denouement.

"It happened—with a vengeance! I went up to Amiens early. A short while before train time, Yvonne appeared. She had driven to the station with an old town official. I stayed in the background until she got on the train.

"She looked awfully sweet and was wearing one pair of the stockings I brought her. As soon as we moved out of the station, I started looking her up. I had watched where she got on. She was surely glad to see me. We stood in the passageway a moment.

"The train was loaded to the guards with soldiers going on leave to Paris. She didn't have much to say and I didn't either. She seemed to be waiting for something. Presently, I heard a voice behind us speaking English. She turned around and in the next moment was in the arms of an English Lieutenant. His name was either Rice or Ross or Moss, I don't remember. But she said, 'Lieutenant Hall, I want you to meet my fiancé,' and the young Englishman blushed and went to shaking hands.

"The fiancé let the cat out of the bag when he said, 'Well, now, I say, this took some planning, didn't it?' I told them good-bye and spent the rest of the trip looking out the window. The idea of that naïve little devil slipping one over like that. Of course, I had to make the trip anyhow, but then I had more or less planned on a bit of romance, and with Yvonne romance would surely be possible."

In Paris, on his brief leave before he picked up a new plane to take back to his squadron, Bert ran into Lufbery, who was now a major in the United States Air Service and in command of two American squadrons stationed at Villeneuve, outside of Paris.

"I told Luf about how little Yvonne two-timed me, and he said, 'Well, it serves you right. You had no business trying to ruin a high school girl.' I said, 'Ruin, hell! What about the Englishman, the fiancé?' 'Oh,' he said, 'they don't count in the life of a young woman; they're so brotherly.' But I don't take any stock in that."

During the course of an evening that began at the New York Bar, which Hall described as being "so full of Americans I could hardly get in the front door," Hall introduced himself and Lufbery to a Frenchwoman named Paulette. The next day he wrote this in his diary:

"Mlle. Paulette and her partner Imogen cheered both of us up later. Luf said to me during the evening, 'Bert, that Paulette girl has the most beautiful chassis I ever saw in my life.' And I said, 'Follow me around, lad, I know how to pick 'em.' And he said, 'Yes, you old bastard, like the little school girl up there at Amiens,' and he made a nasty noise at me through his fist."

As both men finished up the duties that brought them to Paris, they had lunch in the arcade off the Boulevard des Italiens before heading to their respective airfields.

"I asked Luf what he supposed would happen to us after the war—what would we work at, etc.? He said, 'Work at! After the war?' 'Why,' he said, 'who the hell expects there will be any "after the war" anyhow?' And he kept sayin', '"After the war" for aviators!'"

Back at the front, Hall made this diary entry:

"Over to Yvonne's to dinner tonight, and she was there—a little sadder but a lot wiser, perhaps. She is scared stiff that I will say something to her aunt that would let the secret out. The old girl does not know anything about the fiancé. Yvonne said she would explain the entire affair some time, but just now she couldn't talk about it. I said, 'Same stockings?' She said, 'Yes, I saved them while I was away.' And to prove it, she pulled up her skirt and showed me the top of the one she had cut off. It had been all sewed over to prevent it from raveling. Lufbery's statement about Mlle. Paulette's beautiful chassis applies to Yvonne too. She's a beautiful baby. I wish she could be interested in one man at a time. I suggested this to the little devil, but she said, 'C'est la guerre.'

"The fiancé's name is Lieutenant Brewster-Price—a double name and he seems to be more than just an ordinary Limey cockney. Yvonne says the 'Leftenant' means to do right by her and marry her. Lufbery was right about the Englishmen as lovers. The 'Leftenant's' family is rich, but he is a machine-gunner. Too bad!"

Hall's life continued precariously, with days in combat at the front, and the relief of an occasional visit to Yvonne. He noted this emotional seesaw a month after he met Yvonne. Referring to a narrow escape in a dogfight, he said of the enemy bullets that hit his new plane, "I came off with several well-placed patterns of machine gun fire, any one of which might have abbreviated my life, but Yvonne's stocking top did the trick this time. That sweet little devil! I was mistaken about the stocking coming off the wrong leg . . . I saw her a little while tonight. She says she is worried about the Left-enant; that is Price, the machine-gunner. According to her story, he was going into the lines near Ribécourt. How she found this out, God only knows, and if the Leftenant wrote it to her, I surely have no faith in British censorship. But anyhow, Ribécourt is in that bulge in the lines just a little this side of Cambrai. I looked it up on the Headquarters' map, and I don't think much of the Leftenant's chances if the Boche start a push, because that will naturally be straight-ened out and the machine-gunner Leftenant will naturally be straightened out with it. But, oh, hell, I tried to get her to stick to an aviator. She *would* go and get herself mixed up with a really hazardous branch of the service."

In mid-March, Hall came down with a severe cold. Recovering to some extent, he learned that Russia had signed a peace treaty: "That will free all those divisions on the Eastern Front, and now those smart Boche will trans-port all those free divisions over here to pester us . . . Saw Yvonne tonight a while. She is worried frightful about her man. I said why not have a man she could depend on, but she said I didn't understand, and then she went into the café crying. It's serious!"

A few days later, what Hall had foreseen occurred.

"It happened. Up at Headquarters, they told us that the artillery bombardment started at 5.00 a.m. on a front of more than sixty miles . . . By sundown tonight the Boche had penetrated five miles everywhere, except at Flesquières. That's where Yvonne's lover is located, and may the Lord have pity on him!"

Hall added that "the air is alive with German planes," and that Richthofen's famous "Squadron 11 is opposite us."

A day later, Hall wrote this: "When I told Yvonne that the place where her lover had been is now in German hands, she screamed and carried on something terrible. The poor little thing is pregnant by him. She said the child should be born in September; that's why she had been ill recently."

As for his own situation, he said that "my throat is worse and my plane is shot to hell. Only made one patrol. The casualties in our group are too awful to recount . . . It is rumored at Headquarters that the German divisions involved in this offensive are dying off like flies from a new disease called 'influenza'; some call it 'Spanish influenza.'"

On March 24, seven weeks after he met Yvonne, Bert made this grim diary entry:

"Everything is shot to hell . . . the Fifth British Army is practically out of the war. Twenty-five kilometers lost in three days! And it took months to gain 500 meters in some places.

"We have moved back. I told Yvonne good-bye and begged her to pack her stuff and come on, but she would not leave the old woman and the old woman believes that the war will never get to her again. So here they are—those two defenseless females—and they won't leave."

A few hours later: "From the air, I saw some activity around Yvonne's place . . . they must still be there."

Three days after this, Hall once again mixed military intelligence, his deteriorating physical and mental health, and his thoughts of Yvonne.

"A German dispatch picked up and sent to Headquarters says that seventy-five Allied planes have been accounted for in five days . . . the bombardment is coming closer all the time. Yvonne's place still seems to be going; at least, it is from the air. My throat is getting better, but I'm getting mighty tired. With the casualties we are having, I don't see how I can expect to last it out."

Two days after that, the curtain started coming down.

"Today I flew over the spot where Yvonne's place used to be. It was just at sundown. The artillery bombardment has completely obliterated any trace of the cottage where she had her café. And Yvonne! I wonder! Poor pregnant little devil! And the Leftenant—just a month ago now those two were in Paris . . . God, I'm weary! I wish it was all over. Somehow, I believe I've had enough."

Then: "March 30. If they still want to send me to the hospital I think I'll let 'em do it tomorrow. The offensive is nearly over and Yvonne's gone and I'm ready for a rest."

Later: "Hospital O. K., food good, beds soft, girls pretty, cigarettes plentiful, war still going on."

Discharged from the hospital, on April 12 he wrote, "I am still groggy. Took off a little while today to try my hand. The news from the north is still disquieting. Flew over the place where Yvonne's cottage used to be. The ground is absolutely smooth. I'm going to get one of the men in the adjoining photographic sections to take an aerial picture of the place, so as to be sure I'm not mistaken."

Bert Hall mentioned Yvonne just twice more. On May 22, a hundred and two days after he first saw her, he made this diary entry.

"Over to Paillart, where the Yanks have one of their Field Hospitals—it's No. 3, I believe—there is a little girl who reminds me of Yvonne. When I first saw her the other day I nearly dropped dead, but I was mistaken. Just the same, she made some very soft eyes at me. It isn't worth while working up a friendship with her though, because there are too many American doctors and hospital sergeants around to put up competition. The little peach runs a pastry shop. Her name is Edith and she can't be over nineteen."

There is an interesting tone in Hall's reference to "the Americans" or "the Yanks" in this and his other diary entries of that time, as if Americans had a separate nationality from his own, and yet he never identifies himself as being French. Perhaps the war, and its uncompromising nature, made him a man without a country.

Bert Hall had a bit of unfinished business.

"Yesterday I went out to the Passy district and visited with Mother Pivot who used to be the concierge and took care of my apartment. Her son Philip went away with the first mobilization in August, 1914. He was going to the Beaux-Arts and studying to be an architect. Mother Pivot was still there, but very bent and very sad. Philip never came back. He was last seen somewhere up near Charleroi [Belgium]. I gave the old girl a present and came away sadder than before."

Twenty-seven

Good-Bye, Luf.
And Thank You.

By May of 1918 Major Raoul Lufbery was assigned to the United States 94th Aero Squadron, known for its famous "Hat-in-the-Ring" insignia depicting a red, white, and blue top hat inside a circle. At this point Lufbery had sixteen confirmed kills. In addition to helping break in new pilots, he was authorized to fly by himself whenever he had time to go hunting for unsuspecting German planes.

On the morning of May 19, a German photo-reconnaissance plane came into view above his squadron's base. The only pilot on the ground ready to "scramble" and intercept the lumbering three-seater enemy plane, a Rumpler, was a lieutenant who had never flown in combat.

Lufbery came out of a squadron building to watch how the fledgling American pilot would handle himself. He saw the novice open fire from too great a distance, nervously keeping up a long burst that probably used up all his ammunition, while the intruder, now receiving antiaircraft fire, started to head back to the German lines.

Deciding to get into the air and take charge of the situation, Lufbery leapt onto a motorcycle and raced down to the hangars. Shrugging into his flight suit, he learned that his own plane was not ready to fly, and climbed into another one, taking off without his usual meticulous check of the machine guns.

Catching up on the slower enemy plane while keeping an eye out for German fighters that might ambush the inexperienced American pilot, Lufbery fired several short bursts before his guns jammed. He broke off contact, cleared the jam, and then slid into position to attack the enemy plane from the rear.

His plane staggered in the air, struck by a round fired by the observer seated facing backward in the rear seat of the enemy plane. The bullet had come through his fuel tank, setting it afire and cutting off the thumb of his right hand, which had been gripping the control stick.

Lufbery tried to put his falling plane into a sideslipping maneuver that would keep the spreading flames away from him—a movement that had been known to extinguish such a fire—but this failed. He climbed out onto a wing, but flames from the body of the plane reached out and set his flight suit on fire. Lufbery spotted a stream two thousand feet below him that might conceivably break his fall and save his life by plunging him into water.

He leapt, landing a hundred yards from the water and fatally impaling himself on a vegetable garden fence made of rough, vertically arranged logs with sharpened tops. In a photograph taken soon after his death, a French peasant woman stands in front of the fence holding a large, wrapped-up fragment of wood that she removed from Lufbery's throat as she pulled his body off the spike-ended logs.

Everywhere Hall saw American units moving up to the front for the great final offensives, but his best memories were of the war's early days. He flew over the little village where he had met and started his dalliance with Yvonne, and found the village leveled, with no sign of where the restaurant had stood. He made the laconic diary entry, "Yvonne has disappeared." He knew that Lufbery's latest girlfriend had died of the influenza epidemic now sweeping around the world. The office housing American aviation headquarters in Paris was filled with fliers veterans like him called "kiwis": birds that had wings but never flew. As for the fate of many Americans who had fought at the front, he wrote of a day in 1918 when he visited what he called "the American 5th Hospital," located in the infield of the thoroughbred racetrack at Auteuil on the outskirts of Paris. What stuck in his mind were "the rolls of bloody bandages under those hot tents," but he had a worse experience than that.

"At the Bacouel dressing station I saw two Yank boys who had been burned with a 'flammenwerfer' [flame-thrower] . . . Those things shoot a hot burning stuff like tar, and these poor boys were in a terrible condition. One of them was completely insane. He screamed every time anyone made the slightest noise. A doctor told me that neither one of them could possibly live because of the great area of skin affected by the burning. When they took their clothes off, skin, flesh, and all came off in some places.

"Two mothers will get flowery notes from the War Department saying that God decided to call Willie and Charlie home to be with the angels, and the boys will be put away in a grave with a wooden cross on top."

Twenty-eight

Different American Wings in French Skies

On October 3, 1918, roughly five weeks before the war ended, five hundred American soldiers were surrounded in the Argonne Forest by a greatly superior German force. This isolated unit, which became known as the "Lost Battalion," was part of the 77th Division, all New Yorkers, whose shoulder patch depicted the Statue of Liberty. Their commander was a scholarly, bespectacled peacetime lawyer named Charles Whittlesey. They were out of food and ammunition, and more of them were being killed or wounded every hour.

By the next day, only 190 men were left. In addition to the fire being poured down on them by the Germans holding higher ground, American artillery units were mistakenly shelling their area, increasing their casualties.

With all other forms of communication cut off, Whittlesey turned to the three messenger pigeons his unit had with them. If one of these birds could get through to the loft at division headquarters to which it had been trained to return when released, the surviving members of this unit might yet be saved.

Each bird had a small metal cylinder attached to one of its legs, into which a rolled-up message could be put.

The first bird, carrying the message, "Many wounded. We cannot evacuate," went up in the air. By now all of Whittlesey's men were crowded into a small area, and everyone knew that the bird was carrying what could be their only hope of survival. The Germans shot the bird down.

Whittlesey sent off a second bird, carrying the message, "Men are suffering. Can support be sent?" In full view of everyone, it too was killed in flight and came plunging to earth.

The third bird, mistakenly listed as being a male and named "Cher Ami," was readied for flight. In the cylinder on her left leg was placed this last desperate note:

"We are along the road parallel to 276.4. Our own artillery is dropping a barrage directly on us. For heaven's sake stop it."

As Cher Ami rose into view, the Germans fired at her a number of times before she, too, was hit. She went down, "shot through the breast, blinded in one eye, covered in blood and with a leg hanging by only a tendon." She struggled into the air again, and managed to get to division headquarters, twenty-five miles away, in only sixty-five minutes. Her message stopped the lethal "friendly fire" bombardment, and, now knowing where the remnants of the "Lost Battalion" were, a strong relief column fought their way through and saved them.

Army surgeons worked hard to save the heroic pigeon's life. Unable to save her nearly severed leg, they carved a wooden leg for her. When Cher Ami was well enough to be sent to the United States on a ship, General Pershing was there to salute her as she was taken aboard.

Back in America, she received two medals, including the French *Croix de Guerre*. She died a few months later, as a result of her wounds. Taxidermists prepared her body and she was placed in an honored position in a display case in the Smithsonian Institution. To this day, she remains in the Smithsonian's National Museum of History's "Price of Freedom" exhibit.

Twenty-nine

The End of a Long Four Years

At the beginning of Bert Hall's last entry in the diary he began during the war, there are the italicized words, referring to a famous French ocean liner, "*On the Rochambeau— enroute to America*." What compounds the confusion about his whereabouts in 1918 is that he stopped dating his diary entries on May 28. Although the assumption is that this ship was steaming westward across the Atlantic, it is hard to know just when the voyage occurred. There is no question that at some point during the last year of the war he was busy in Ithaca, New York—then a center of the silent film industry—rewriting his book "*En l'Air!*" to be made into a film titled *A Romance of the Air*. Not surprisingly, he cast himself as the hero and played that part in the movie. The film was played in many theaters around the country, always in conjunction with a personal appearance by him. By coincidence, he appeared on Broadway in Manhattan's Rivoli Theatre on Armistice Day, November 11, 1918. The

New York Times said of the movie, "It is highly melodramatic, but includes a number of excellent scenes of airplane activity." The *New-York Tribune*'s review included this: "This picture is interesting mainly because one knows much of what happens on the screen is true. It is a story of spies and miraculous escapes, and even if Dulcinea did say it, 'Truth is stranger than fiction.'"

In any case, whether he was on the *Rochambeau* or had already crossed the Atlantic, his diary entry said this:

"It seems to be all over. People salute me and speak very respectfully. They make me feel like somebody, but I'm not here at all. I'm really back there in the Champagne [fighting in the Foreign Legion] or up in the Chemin des Dames, or beside Jim McConnell in his little grave at Ham, or down at Nancy with the only honest-to-God aviator the Americans have produced—Raoul Lufbery!"

A slogan at the time of the Armistice called the fighting from 1914 to 1918 "The War to End War," but things occurred that cast a different shadow.

At the war's close, the German "Flying Circus" commander Hermann Goering and his pilots destroyed their planes so that the Allies could not use them. On the night their unit was disbanded, its survivors gathered in a restaurant in a town near Frankfurt, where the final paperwork for processing out of the German Army had been done. One of the pilots remembered the officers' party that night.

"At one point in the evening Hermann climbed onto the little bandstand with a glass in his hand, and although everyone was shouting and roistering there was something in his manner that made us all suddenly silent. He began to speak. He hardly raised his voice at all, but there was a strange quality to it, an emotional underbeat, that seemed to slip through the chinks in your flesh and reach right into your heart. He spoke of the Richthofen squadron and what it had done, of how its achievements, the skill and bravery of its pilots, had made it famous the world over."

Goering asked them to look to the future. The pilot recounting the occasion said that Goering closed his talk to his men with this: "Our time will come again." Then he raised his glass and said, "Gentlemen, I give you a toast— 'To the Fatherland and to the Richthofen squadron.' He drank and then smashed his glass down at his feet, and we all did likewise. Many of us were weeping, Hermann among them."

Thirty

L'Envoi—Farewell

The Lafayette Escadrille and its pilots did many things that had many results, but in the end, for them it was all about flying. The skies drew those men to them like moths to a flame. The idealists loved to fly; the adventurers loved to fly; the gamblers, engineers, race car drivers, writers, athletes—they all loved to fly.

The Escadrille received many epitaphs, but no tribute more fitting than the final words bestowed upon his comrades by Bert Hall. A cad, a con man, a spy, a wise man, a wounded hero, he wrote:

"War is a silly business, but there never was a time when the last bit of manhood came out as it came out with our gang at the front."

Fig 22. The Lafayette Escadrille Memorial on the outskirts of Paris. Forty-six American fliers are buried there. The memorial is modeled on the Arc de Triomphe in Paris and is approximately half that monument's size.

Acknowledgments

First, I want to praise the wonderful work done on my behalf by my wife, Katherine Burnam Flood. She has supported my efforts in every possible way.

I also wish to thank my children: my daughter, Lucy Flood, a published writer herself, who accompanied me in 2013 on a nine-day research trip to France in connection with this book; my son Caperton, who has been a great help to me in a number of ways, including providing some terrific edits to this book and spending a couple of priceless weeks with me at its completion; and my son Curtis, who helped me conceive of this work and who was enormously useful to me in driving me to Saratoga Springs, New York, on a research trip to see the Grant Cottage, which figured prominently in my last book, *Grant's Final Victory*.

I wish also to express my admiration for my daughter Lucy's husband, Kirill Kireyev, an immigrant from Belarus who received his BA from Cornell University, as well as a doctorate in cognitive science and computer science from the University of Colorado. He has distinguished himself in a number of ways, including founding the prize-winning educational research engine instaGrok. My daughter-in-laws Jera and Christine have also been helpful in the whole family effort.

The next person I wish to thank is Dwight Taylor, a successful corporate lawyer. He assisted me greatly as an undergraduate at Harvard, then continued this support on some of my more recent books. I put to him my desire for his help on everything from concepts to commas.

My longtime friend Thomas J. Fleming, author of more than forty books, has repeatedly helped me in improving my work.

Next I wish to thank Betina Gardner, dean of the splendid library at Eastern Kentucky University, where I have an office. She and any number of her able and dedicated staff have always led from in front.

I am deeply grateful to my assistant, Carol Tudor Thomas, of the Collections and Discovery Department, who has taken home hundreds of pages of my work to read and often improved them on her own time.

Over the years at the library, I have enjoyed some lively lunches with the library's Lunch Club that have brightened my days. The club's members include Stefanie Brooks of Interlibrary Loan; Judy Warren of Circulation; Beverly Hisel, Circulation; Anna Collister, the administrative assistant to the dean; Leah Banks, Reference Services; Tessa Berry of Circulation; and Eric Hall of Circulation.

Some of the staff who have given me the most assistance with research are Kevin Jones, Rob Sica, and Linda Sizemore—all Reference librarians—and Pat New, retired from Interlibrary Loan. Numerous custodians have helped me keep my office bright and cheery, and I have always enjoyed the crew at Java City, EKU Library's in-house coffee shop.

Amber Smith of Richmond, Kentucky, has provided me with many original and useful research materials. Professor Carroll Hale, of Eastern Kentucky University's Department of Art and Art History, has supplied excellent maps for the book. I am grateful to Cindy Trainor Blyberg for her work on the photo layouts.

I have had successful research trips to the libraries of Washington and Lee University, the University of Virginia, and the College of William and Mary.

Bridget Saltonstall of Concord, Massachusetts, has been very helpful to me on this book and others. Thomas Parrish, the author of many excellent books, who lives in nearby Berea, Kentucky, has assisted me greatly with several of my manuscripts. My old friend Sidney Offit, of New York City, has often helped me with my work. My friend Marilyn Heineman also provided me with valuable reflections on the book.

Writer and researcher Edward C. Pulliam of Alexandria, Virginia, has frequently aided me with projects involving the Washington, D.C., area.

Among those who helped me greatly on my research trip to Paris are Maxime de Taisne, Van Kirk Reeves, and my old friend Edouard Emmett. Former ambassador to Luxembourg James G. Lowenstein was also helpful to me. Mme. Wilks Brocard, daughter of Antonin Brocard, the postwar chief of the French Air Force, was most pleasant in sharing some of her memories and extending kindness to my daughter Lucy. My friend Martin "Yukata" Nomachi, a colleague and true friend from my days teaching at Sophia University in Tokyo between 1963 and 1965, joined us in Paris to attend ceremonies at the Lafayette Escadrille Memorial, which is a half-sized copy of the Arc de Triomphe located eight miles from the center of Paris.

In recent years, I have been exceptionally fortunate in having the literary representation of John Taylor "Ike" Williams, being very ably assisted by Hope Denekamp, and benefiting from the extremely helpful editing of Katherine Flynn. I feel privileged to have as my publisher Grove/ Atlantic Monthly Press, where my editor is Joan Bingham, helped by Jamison Stoltz and Allison Malecha.

Notes

In citing works in the notes, short titles have generally been used. Works frequently cited have been identified by the following abbreviations. The full citation appears in the bibliography, under the name of the author or editor.

ASW	Alice S. Weeks, *Greater Love Hath No Man*
BH	Bert Hall, *"En l'Air!"*
BHN	Bert Hall and John Jacob Niles, *One Man's War*
BP	Blaine Pardoe, *The Bad Boy*
DG	Dennis Gordon, *Lafayette Escadrille Pilot Biographies*
E	Edwin C. Parsons, *I Flew with the Lafayette Escadrille*
E1	Edwin C. Parsons, *Flight into Hell*
E2	Edwin C. Parsons, *The Great Adventure*
G	Edmond Charles Clinton Genet and Walt Brown, *An American for Lafayette*
JHN	James Norman Hall, Charles Nordhoff, and Edgar G. Hamilton, *The Lafayette Flying Corps*
NYT	*New York Times*

One—By God I Know Mighty Well What I Would Do!

Herrick's meeting, ending with "took service in the Foreign Legion" Mott, *Herrick,* 143–145.

Two days after the war began. Mason, *Lafayette Escadrille,* 5.

"They filed into my office" Mott, 143

"I think the people of the United States" Ibid. 144.

"We weren't fooled" BHN, 25.

"Our consciences demanded it" Ibid. 25.

Two—How the New Thing Grew

"With only slight exaggeration" E1, 42.

"baby carriages" E2, 165.

"truck drivers" Ibid. 130.

"The airplane is all very well" Mason, 17.

The September 6 date conforms to a Wikipedia article that says in part, "Utilizing the new technology of aviation, Allied reconnaissance planes quickly spotted this gap and reported it to Joffre." militaryhistory.about.com/od/worldwari/p/World-War-I-First-Battle-Of-The-Marne.htm

Flammer, *The Knighted Skies,* 29, describes the contribution to the "Miracle of the Marne" made by British pilots who radioed the location of German forces to Allied artillery units. The overall strategic situation can be found in Mason, 7, 9.

"I was blithely flying" Von Richthofen's duel with Hawker. Von Richthofen, *The Red Fighter Pilot,* 105.

"My father discriminates" Ibid. 153.

Three—Aspects of the Great New Dimension

"He was one of that famed band" E2, 17. Bach's exploits on his ill-fated spy mission are in E2, 22–29, and the title given him by the Germans is in Hall, James Norman, *The Lafayette Flying Corps,* I, 100–101.

Four—What Manner of Men?

"The top fitted over the skull" E2, 236.

"War aviators individually" E2, 224–232.

"a salute or wave" E2, 25.

"well-known ace" E1, 193.

Paul Rockwell delivers the bourbon, DG, 51.

"the startling success" E2, 7

"'The Bottle of Death'" E2, 7.

"At the Gare St. Lazare" BHN, 29.

Five—Contrasts

"We all eat together" and "I am sitting by my window" DG, 50.

"I didn't pay any attention" DG, 50.

"All Luxeuil smiled upon him" DG, 51.

"Kiffin was a popular hero" BHN, 132.

"a tremendous wave of excitement" DG, 51.

"Now, 'K,' what will you do?" Jablonski, *The Knighted Skies,* 39.

Thaw: four bridges and other feats. DG, 55.

Thaw and *Imperator.* DG, 55.

"a burly brute" E, 89.

"One day" BP, 55, citing Flammer, *The Vivid Air,* 9.

A German who spoke. E1, 13.

F. C. Hild Mason, 43.

"You must be" BP, 67.

Much about the activities of Gros and Thaw is to be found in Rogers' *L'Escadrille Lafayette,* 3.

German secret service agents. E2, 15.

Bernstorff's encounter with Thaw in Flammer, *The Vivid Air,* 25; also Mason, *The Lafayette Escadrille,* 53.

"they had created" E2, 15.

Influence of Verdun. Mason, 53.

Six—The Odds Are Never Good: Clyde Balsley

"Five feet eleven" Dunbar, *The Swallow,* 129.

"see the war, and see it well" DG, 87.

"something struck me" This and the subsequent descriptions and quotations involving Balsley are from DG, 88–91.

"You know we didn't" Ibid. 89.

"A German was at my left" through "bleeding like a pig" Ibid. 88.

"Two took me by the shoulders" DG, 89.

"Jacques," he gasped. Ibid. 91.

"My cry for water was so intense" Ibid. 43.

Seven—The Oddsmaker Is Impersonal: Victor Chapman

E2, 104, refers him as the "best beloved pilot of the Escadrille Americaine."

"whom everyone in our squad[ron] loved deeply" Ibid. 37.

"a lover of art" BH, 152–153.

"There is no question" JHN, II, 226.

"The next morning I woke" through 'But I'm not going to die.'" JHN, II, 65–66.

"If Victor is killed" *NYT,* June 25, 1916.

"My son's life" *NYT,* June 4, 1916.

"the living symbol" DG, 38.

"Never in my country . . ." Jusserand's speech. *NYT,* September 7, 1916.

"Although, after the removal . . ." E1, 103.

Eight——Women at War: Alice Weeks

"We are somewhere on the ocean" Weeks, *Greater Love Hath No Man,* 16.

"when we landed" Ibid. 17.

"By the time I reached the train" Ibid. 18.

". . . the stories I hear" Ibid. 23.

"We know that" Weeks, Kenneth, *Science, Sentiments and Senses,* 49.

"It is commencing to grow cold" Weeks, *Greater Love Hath No Man,* 6.

"They have destroyed" Ibid. 5.

"Big attack here" Ibid. 22.

"My dear, I embrace you" Ibid. 7.

"Much love, dear" Ibid. 13.

"Yesterday we had" Ibid. 40.

"I am working at St. Sulpice" Ibid. 23.

"Today I sent" Ibid. 32.

"I have thirty men" Ibid. 125.

"had adventures" Ibid. 47.

Café brawl. Ibid. 98.

"Kill me quick" Ibid. 101.

"eighteen months at the front" Ibid. 110.

"A French soldier came to me" Ibid. 130.

French soldier from Australia. Ibid. 142.

"Also please send me" Ibid. 17.

"Your bug water" Ibid. 18.

"the less to carry" Ibid. 18.

"Have been fighting hard" Ibid. 34.

"Only 1,800 out of 4,000" Ibid. 36.

". . . we have been fighting hard" through "I will stay with my regiment" Ibid. 35.

"Will you find out" Ibid. 41.

"The woman I am supporting" Ibid. 39.

"I have never seen a tear" Ibid. 43.

"This is only a line" Ibid. 45.

"running toward the third line" Ibid. 45.

"He looks terribly" DG, 51.

Lawrence Scanlan. Weeks, 64.

"It is becoming a meeting place" Ibid. 62.

Walbron's story. Ibid. 150.

"My kitten Coco" Ibid. 120.

Body of Kenneth Weeks discovered. Ibid. 45.

"I have been notified" Ibid. 106.

"After all these months" Ibid. 106.

Service for Kenneth. Ibid. 107–108.

Details of the death and burial of Douglas MacMonagle. DG, 227.

Nine—More American Eagles Take to the Sky

A husky French military doctor. The description of the physical is from E2, 35–36.

"The second line" E, 36–37.

"Penguins" Jablonski, *Warriors with Wings*, 61.

"The rest of us" E, 90.

"he asked for a transfer" E1, 49.

Ten—There Was This Man Named Bert Hall

"fourteen were from families of average income" DG, 2.

long thin nose. Sengupta, *Lafayette Escadrille*, 42.

Bowling Green birth date. BH, third page of front matter.

Higginsville date. DG, 69.

Kansas City and Dallas. Gordon, *The Lafayette Flying Corps*, 202.

"I don't think I ever loved" BHN, 301.

"The problem for . . ." Dennis Gordon, in his foreword to BP.

"best eyes in the French Army!" BHN, 60.

"beef up" the diary entries and come up with something longer than the 152-page "*En l'Air!*"; John Jacob Niles and "*One Man's War.*" BP, 130, 140–145, 149, 152, 173, 204–212.

"Bert climbed into the machine" Gordon, *The Lafayette Flying Corps*, 204.

The two agents. BP, 57.

"A volunteer was called for" BHN, 80–81.

"Whole columns of Boche" Ibid. 80–81.

"I never will forget the concierge" Ibid. 21.

Visit to Mother Pivot. Ibid. 112.

"Following the trip to the Invalides" Ibid. 29.

Eleven—New Commanders for a New Form of Combat

"We are here" Rogers, *L'Escadrille Lafayette,* Chapter 6, 25.

"From the point of view" Mason, 128.

The two pilots who wrote of their appreciation for Thenault's handling of his pilots were Ned Parsons and Harold Willis. DG, 240–241.

"Thenault would invariably . . ." DG, 241. A similar account is in E2, 266.

Thenault at Le Plessis-Belleville. Ibid. 240.

"in spite of his handicaps" Ibid. 101.

"Mon Capitaine, it is a new invention" BHN, 150.

Twelve—Shadows of War in the "City of Light"

"For a woman to dress brightly" Gordon, 25.

Holt bumps into Melvin. Ibid. 423.

"There will be no end of artificial legs needed" DG, 159.

"Paris is beautiful now" Weeks, 150.

"The Dance of the Chastity Belts" BHN, 214.

Pilots, 22 Rue de Berri, and Henry Jones. DG, 25, and Gordon, *The Lafayette Flying Corps,* 266.

Thirteen—Things Are Different Up There, and Then on the Ground

Only four bullets. E5.

The incident of the French pilot deliberately crashing into the German plane. McConnell, *Flying for France,* 123.

"Suddenly, out of the corner of my eye" E2, 132.

"[They] must have been" Ibid.

"to whom trouble" DG, 194.

Campbell. Accounts of the episode of the locked-together planes are in DG, 195–196, E 2, 268–269, and Jablonski, 168–169.

"did not put the plane" Weeks, 109.

"unheard-of luxury" and "was delighted to accept" Parsons, E1, 194.

"Take a ship up" E2, 219.

High-altitude gear. JHN, II, 58.

"We also carry oxygen tubes" BH, 99.

"Feet were twin lumps" E2, 220.

"When I say necessity" and the half-pint flask. Ibid. 219.

"the food of the nerves" DG, 19.

"Few people" E2, 211.

"I set my wheels" Ibid. 216.

"I wasn't sleeping nights" Ibid. 219.

"Sober, I'm a nervous" DG, 4. This was said by Captain Elliott White Springs, who wrote numerous pieces about his experience, including the book *War Birds*.

"None of us had any real idea" E2, 8–10.

"There was no one" Charles Dolan quotation, on the frontispiece of DG. There he is misidentified as Carl Dolan.

"Our adversaries in the air" E2, 192.

Fourteen—Bert Hall Takes Life by the Horns

"When we passed over" BHN, 86–87.

"were given orders" Ibid. 191.

"When we got back to the field" Ibid. 191–192.

Fifteen—Aces

"Broad forehead" E2, 73.

Lufbery's meeting and association with Pourpe. Jablonski, 98–99.

"He was a walking encyclopedia" BHN, 162.

"I only know one" E2, 73.

Lufbery and mushrooms. DG, 84, quoting Hinkle.

"He spent hours" E2, 78.

"He had a happy faculty" Ibid.

"so thoroughly shot up" McConnell, Flying for France, 102.

"two bullets went through" E2, 79.

"four neat bullet holes" Ibid. 82–83.

"His air work was incomparable" Ibid. 77.

"To fly high" Thenault, The Story of the Lafayette Escadrille, 124.

"dominate the situation" DG, 82.

Incident at Chartres. Rogers, L'Escadrille Lafayette, Chapter 6, 38, citing Journal: Escadrille No. 124; DG, 84; Flammer, The Vivid Air, 140, citing Journal de Marche of June 3–6, 1916; Jablonski, 114.

"When flames burst" BHN, 177.

"We hadn't been in Paris two hours" BHN, 180.

"Whiskey" In BP, 92–93, there is a different version of how the lion cub got his name.

"When Whiskey was a year old" E2, 149.

"They are known" DG, 168–169; the pilot quoted is James Norman Hall.

"Can I fly that?" through "a mask of horror" Mason, *High Flew the Falcons,* 118–133.

"A wonderful chap" DG, 246.

Nungesser's aggressive attacking. Mason, 118–133.

Sixteen—A Bloody Report Card

"From what I have observed" BHN, 167–170.

"It seemed to us on the front" E2, 33.

". . . Like dueling" Lewis, *Sagittarius Rising,* 170.

Udet's entry into the German Army Air Service. en.wikipedia.org/wiki/Ernst_Udet

"The fuselage of the Farman" through "You would actually seem ripe for us" en.wikipedia.org/wiki/Farman_F.30

Life expectancy of fifteen hours in the air. E2, 32.

Seventeen—Bert Hall as Thinker, Bartender, and Raconteur

"It's bad for the troops" BHN, 166–167.

Hall's wound, June 26, 1917. Recorded in Thenault's logbook of all flights by Lafayette Escadrille pilots. BHN, 154

Hall sees shot-down pilot. BHN, 326.

Thaw's wound. BHN, 141.

"With me the great trouble is" BH, 3.

"One afternoon" BHN, 183–187.

Eighteen—Bad Things Happen to Good New Men
Indian Head insignia. Jablonski, 137–138; DG, 176.

"to fly to Chartres" DG, 173

"I tried photographic work" DG, 172.

"With his trained and intelligent brain" DG, 173.

"This pilot who" through "a long time afterwards" DG, 173–175.

Nineteen—Convenient Emergencies
"just cut out for good and all" E2, 65.

"hanging head down" Ibid. 65–66.

"He pushed up all right" through "I was the other" Ibid. 66.

"That was a great gag" BHN, 172.

Twenty—Unique Volunteers
Biographical material on Kenneth Marr. This is a combination of what is to be found in DG, 177, and in Flammer, *The Vivid Air,* 120. Reading both of these sources leaves unresolved the question of whether it was Marr or his partner who actually delivered the dogs to the French. Since Flammer, 220, cites his having had an interview with Marr in September of 1960 and speaks of Marr as having brought "some dog teams to France for use in the Vosges Mountains," I favor Marr's account on this point.

"I certainly felt sorry" Gordon, 317.

"I want you all to be good children" Lloyd, *Eugene Bullard,* 11.

"never be happy" Ibid. 36.

"The whole front" Ibid. 43.

"knew damn well" Ibid. 52.

The ceremony at the Arc de Triomphe. www.airpower.maxwell.af.mil/apjinternational/apj-s/2005/3tri05/chivaletteeng.html

Twenty-one—The War Changes Men and Women, Some for Better, and Some for Worse

Rumsey blinds Whiskey in one eye. DG, 99–100.

Effects of blinding Whiskey, and cumulative effects of alcoholism and combat stress on Rumsey Ibid. 100.

"You couldn't walk a block in Paris" DG, 160.

"No one thinks" Ibid. 52.

We are very unlucky" Ibid. 51–52.

Details of this posthumous rivalry are in Ibid. 62, 63, 139, 140.

Oberndorf mission. Jablonski, *Warriors with Wings*, 128–134.

Twenty-two—Colorful Men Arrive on the Eastern Front

"He was with" BHN, 173.

"Aviators in groups" BP, 104.

"He was genial . . ." Ibid. 104.

"After having served" Ibid. 88.

"Clever, energetic" DG, 75.

"Early in December . . ." BH, 16.

'show the Russians" Ibid. 108.

"I hope my messages" BHN, 230.

"asked me questions" Ibid. 230.

"We had dinner" through "coming from a Russian Grand Duke" Ibid. 230–231.

Out of the 1,600 men. BP, 111–112.

Thousands of Romanians Ibid. 112.

"The cold was intense" Ibid.

"lost his job" Ibid. 113.

"Everyone was arrested about twice daily" Ibid. 116.

Leon Trotsky. BHN, 253–254.

Ship's manifest BP, 117 and 208, n.33. It is possible that the *Korea Maru* took him to Shanghai, where he boarded another ship, bound for San Francisco.

Twenty-three—A Letter from Home, to a Young Man with a Secret

Pilot Ned Parsons. Corrections of this account can be found in the website, www.scuttlebuttsmallchow.com/geneted.html. The account nonetheless faithfully portrays the situation described.

"The simple truth" DG, 149.

"with ice all around" Genet, *An American for Lafayette,* 161.

"Fine day but" Ibid. 138.

"Those two I'm convinced" Ibid. 174.

"If I die" Lafayette Escadrille Memorial Restoration brochure, "Preserving the Legacy, Honoring the Airmen," 7.

[This entire account by Norman Hall is cited by Sengupta as being from JHN, II, 16–17.]

Twenty-four—The United States Enters the War

"I left the parade . . ." JHN, II, 17.

". . . 51 were obsolete" BP, 118.

Dudley Hill. DG, 101–104.

Studies concerning placement of squadrons and importance of parity or superiority. "Air Power: United States Participation in World War I" U.S. Centennial of Flight Commission, 2. Also, Sando, Major Terrance, "American Fighter Combat During WWI," Air Command and Staff College, March 1997, Chaper 3, 16.

Twenty-five—A Lion in the Air Passes the Torch, and the Escadrille Bids Its Own Lions Farewell

"Luf and Whiskey were great pals" DG, 170.

Twenty-six—Yvonne!

Everything Bert Hall recounts about his relationship with Yvonne is from his diary entries in BHN, the 1929 Holt edition in which his collaborator is John J. Niles. The pertinent entries begin on page 300, and the final reference to Yvonne is on page 352.

"Of all people" Ibid. 287.

"Everything I learned" DG, 85.

"They have placed me" BHN, 296–297.

"They told me" Ibid.

colored silk stockings. Ibid. 303–313.

"Bert, that Paulette girl" Ibid. 325.

"The ground is absolutely smooth" Ibid. 331.

Twenty-seven—Good-Bye, Luf. And Thank You.

He leapt. DG, 86.

"the rolls of bloody bandages" BHN, 349.

Twenty-nine— The End of a Long Four Years
Movies being made in Ithaca, New York. BP, 127.

Rivoli Theatre appearance, *NYT.* November 11, 1918.

"This picture is interesting" *New York Tribune.* BP, 129.

'Truth is stranger than fiction'" *New York Tribune.* Ibid.

"At one point in the evening" through "Hermann among them" Flood, *Hitler: The Path to Power,* 332, citing page 131 of Rohm, Ernst, *Die geschicte eines hochverraters.* Munich: Verlag Franz Eher Nachfolger, 1928.

Thirty—L'Envoi—Farewell
"War is a silly business" BHN, 353.

Bibliography

www.airpower.maxwell.af.mil/apjinternational/apj-s/2005/ 3tri05/chivaletteeng.html

Bailey, Frank W. and Christophe Cony. *French Air Service War Chronology, 1914–1918: Day-to-Day Claims and Losses by French Fighter, Bomber and Two-Seat Pilots on the Western Front*. London: Grub Street, 2001.

Beatty, Jack. *The Lost History of 1914: Reconsidering the Year the Great War Began*. New York, NY: Walker & Company, 2012.

Brocard, Pierre. *Antonin Brocard*. Bourges, France: Edite par Atout-Livres editions, atoutlivres.com Acheve d'imprimer octbre 2008, Depot legal Paris octobre 2008, ISBN: 978-2-918-023-00-5, EAN: 9782918023005.

Compared Strategy Institute (CSI). Paris, France. www.institut-strategie.fr; www.stratisc.org/Arogers_4.htm

Crăiuţu, Aurelian and Jeffrey C. Isaac. *America Through European Eyes: British and French Reflections on the New World from the Eighteenth Century to the Present*. University Park, PA: Pennsylvania State University Press, 2009.

Cuneo, John R. *Winged Mars*. Harrisburg, PA: Military Service Publishing Company, 1942.

Driggs, Laurence La Tourette. *Heroes of Aviation*. Boston, MA: Little, Brown and Company, 1918.

Dunbar, Ruth. *The Swallow: A Novel Based upon the Actual Experiences of One of the Survivors of the Famous Lafayette Escadrille*. New York, NY: Boni and Liveright, 1919.

en.wikipedia.org/wiki/Ernst_Udet

en.wikipedia.org/wiki/Farman_F.30

Flammer, Philip M. *Primus Inter Pares: A History of the Lafayette Escadrille*. New Haven, CT: Yale University 1963.

———— *The Vivid Air: The Lafayette Escadrille*. Athens, GA: University of Georgia Press, 1981.

Flood, Charles Bracelen. *Hitler: The Path to Power*. Boston, MA: Houghton Mifflin, 1989.

Franks, Norman and Van Wyngarden, Greg. *German Aces of World War I: The Pictorial Record*. Atglen, PA: Schiffer Publishing, Ltd., 2004.

Franks, Norman and Hal Giblin. *Under the Guns of the Kaiser's Aces— Böhme, Müller, von Tutschek and Wolff: The Complete Record of Their Victories and Victims*. London, UK: Grub Street, 2003.

Franks, Norman L. R. and Frank W. Bailey. *Over the Front: A Complete Record of the Fighter Aces and Units of the United States and French Air Services, 1914–1918*. London, UK: Grub Street, 1992.

Franks, Norman and Frank Bailey. *The Storks: The Story of France's Elite Fighter Groupe de Combat 12 (Les Cigognes) in WWI*. London, UK: Grub Street, 1998.

Genet, Edmond Charles Clinton and Walt Brown. *An American for Lafayette: The diaries of E.C.C. Genet, Lafayette Escadrille*. Charlottesville: University Press of Virginia, 1981.

Gordon, Dennis. *Lafayette Escadrille Pilot Biographies*. Missoula, MT: Doughboy Historical Society, 1991.

———— *The Lafayette Flying Corps: The American Volunteers in the French Air Service in World War One*. Atglen, PA: Schiffer Publishing, Ltd., 2000.

Guttman, Jon. SPA124 *Lafayette Escadrille: American Volunteer Airmen in World War I*. Oxford, UK: Osprey Publishing, 2004.

————— *SPAD VII Aces of World War I*. Oxford, UK: Osprey Publishing, 2001.

Hall, Bert. *"En L'Air!" (In the Air): Three Years on and above Three Fronts*. New York, NY: The New Library, Inc., 1918.

Hall, Bert and John Jacob Niles. *One Man's War: The Story of the Lafayette Escadrille*. New York, NY: H. Holt and Co., 1929.

Hall, James Norman. *High Adventure*. New York, NY: Arno Press, 1980.

Hall, James Norman, Charles Nordhoff, and Edgar G. Hamilton. *The Lafayette Flying Corps*. Boston, MA: Houghton Mifflin Company, 1920.

Hanson, Neil. *Unknown Soldiers: The Story of the Missing of the First World War*. New York, NY: Knopf, 2006.

ICARE Revue de L` Aviation Francaise, "L `Escadrille La Fayette," tome 1, no. 3 (1996).

ICARE Revue de L` Aviation Francaise, "L `Escadrille La Fayette," tome 2, no. 1 (1997).

Jablonski, Edward. *The Knighted Skies: A pictorial history of World War I in the Air*. New York, NY: Putnam, 1964.

————— *Warriors with Wings: The Story of the Lafayette Escadrille*. Indianapolis, IN: Bobbs-Merrill, 1966.

Lafayette Escadrille Memorial Testration brochure, "Preserving the Legacy, Honoring the Airmen."

Lewis, Cecil. *Sagittarius Rising*. Alexandria, VA: Time-Life Books, 1991.

Lloyd, Craig. *Eugene Bullard: Black Expatriate in Jazz-Age Paris*. Athens, GA: University of Georgia Press, 2006.

Marix Evans, Martin. *American Voices of World War I: Primary Source Documents, 1917–1920*. London, UK: Fitzroy Dearborn Publishers, 2001.

Mason Jr., Herbert Molloy. *High Flew the Falcons: The French Aces of World War I*. Philadelphia, PA: J.P. Lippincott, 1965.

————— *The Lafayette Escadrille*. New York, NY: Random House, 1964.

McConnell, James R. *Flying for France: With the American Escadrille at Verdun*. New York, NY: Grosset & Dunlap, 1918.

Miller, Roger G. *Like a Thunderbolt: The Lafayette Escadrille and the Advent of American Pursuit in World War I*. Washington, D.C.: Air Force History and Museums Program, 2007.

Moore, Samuel Taylor. *America and the World War: A Narrative of the Part Played by the United States from the Outbreak to Peace*. New York, NY: Greenberg, 1937.

Mott, Thomas Bentley in Myron T. Herrick, ed. *Friend of France: An Autobiographical Biography*. Garden City, NY: Doubleday, Doran & Company, Inc., 1929.

Nichols, Nancy, ed. *Letters Home from the Lafayette Flying Corps*. San Francisco, CA: J. D. Huff and Company, 1993.

Pardoe, Blaine. *The Bad Boy: Bert Hall, Aviator and Mercenary of the Skies*. Oxford, UK: Fonthill Media Limited, 2012.

Parsons, Edwin C. *I Flew with the Lafayette Escadrille*. Indianapolis, IN: E. C. Seale, 1963.

———— *Flight into hell: The Story of the Lafayette Escadrille*. London, UK: J. Long, Limited, 1938.

———— *The Great Adventure: The Story of the Lafayette Escadrille*. Garden City, NY: Doubleday, Doran & Company, Inc., 1937.

Platt, Frank C. *Great Battles of World War I: In the Air*. New York, NY: Weathervane Books, 1966.

Portes, Jacques. *Fascination and Misgivings: The United States in French Opinion, 1870–1914*. Cambridge, UK: Cambridge University Press, 2000.

Powell, Barry B. *Classical Myth*. Upper Saddle River, NJ: Prentice Hall, 2000.

Revell, Alex. *Fall of Eagles: Airmen of World War One*. Barnsley, South Yorkshire, UK: Pen & Sword Aviation, 2011.

Rockwell, Kiffin Yates and Paul Ayres Rockwell. *War Letters of Kiffin Yates Rockwell, Foreign Legionnaire and Aviator, France, 1914–1916*. Garden City, NY: The Country Life Press. 1925.

Rockwell, Paul Ayres. *American Fighters in the Foreign Legion, 1914–1918*. Boston, MA: Houghton Mifflin Company, 1930.

Rosher, Harold. *With the Flying Squadron: Being the War Letters of the Late Harold Rosher to His Family*. New York, NY: Macmillan, 1916.

Sando, Terrance W., American Fighter Combat During WWI, How significant Was America's Late Entry. Ft. Belvoir defense Technical Information Center, March 1997.

www.scuttlebuttsmallchow.com/geneted.html

Sengupta, Narayan. *Lafayette Escadrille: American's Most Famous Squadron*. Red, White and Blue Publishing, 2010.

Taylor, William P. and Francis L. Irvin. *History of the 148th Aero Squadron, Aviation Section, U.S. Army Signal Corps, A.E.F.-B.E.F., 1917–1918*. Lancaster, SC: Tri-County Publishing Co., 1957.

Thayer, Lucien H., Donald Joseph McGee, and Roger James Bender. *America's First Eagles: The Official History of the U.S. Air Service, A.E.F. (1917–1918)*. San Jose, CA: R. J. Bender Publishing, 1983.

Thenault, Georges translated by Walter Duranty. *The Story of the Lafayette Escadrille Told by Its Commander, Captain Georges Thenault*. Boston, MA: Small, Maynard & Co., 1921.

Tuchman, Barbara W. *The Guns of August*. New York, NY: Macmillan, 1962.

———— *The Proud Tower: A Portrait of the World Before the War, 1890–1914*. New York, NY: Macmillan, 1966.

U.S. Centennial of Flight Commission, "United States Participation in World War I."

Von Richthofen, Manfred. *The Red Fighter Pilot: The autobiography of the Red Baron*. St. Petersburg, FL: Red and Black Publishers, 2007.

Walker, Dale L. *Only the Clouds Remain: Ted Parsons of the Lafayette Escadrille*. Amsterdam, NY: Alandale Press, 1980.

Weeks, Alice S. *Greater Love Hath No Man*. Boston, MA: B. Humphries, Inc., 1939.

Weeks, Kenneth. *Science, Sentiments and Senses: A Study in Philosophy*. Ann Arbor, MI: University of Michigan Library, 1914.

Whitehouse, Arch. *Legion of the Lafayette*. Garden City, NY: Doubleday, 1962.

Williams, Oscar. *Immortal Poems of the English Language: British and
American Poetry From Chaucer's Time to the Present Day*. New York,
NY: Pocket Books, 1952.

Willmott, H. P. *World War I*. New York, NY: DK Publishing, 2003.

Illustration Credits

Map by Caroll Hale

Fig 1: WikiCommons

Fig 2: *Paris Herald*, August 26, 1914 (public domain)

Fig 3: National Archives photo no. 242-HB-1103

Figs 4 and 5: Courtesy of the Virginia Military Institute Archives

Fig 6: From Thenault, George. *The Story of the Lafayette Escadrille*. Boston: Small, Maynard & Co., 1921 (public domain)

Fig 7: From McConnell, James R. *Flying for France, With the American Escadrille at Verdun* (1917), on *Documenting the American South*. University Library, University of North Carolina at Chapel Hill

Fig 8: Great War Primary Document Archive: Photos of the Great War (gwpda.org/photos)

Fig 9: Library of Congress

Fig 10: National Air and Space Museum collection, NASM A-48745-R

Fig 11: WikiCommons

Fig 12: WikiCommons

Fig 13: Bildarchiv Austria

Fig 14: National Air and Space Museum, NASM-2005-17461

Fig 15: New England Air Museum

Fig 16: National Air and Space Museum Archives, NASM A-4876-A

Fig 17: Solent News and Photo Agency

Fig 18: Great War Primary Document Archive: Photos of the Great War (gwpda.org/photos)

Fig 19: Credit: Great War Primary Document Archive: Photos of the Great War (www.gwpda.org/photos)

Fig 20: New England Air Museum

Fig 21: © SZ Photo/Scherl/The Image Works

Fig 22: United States Air Force